Hope

and Help

for
Living
with
Illness

Karen Zielinski

Franciscan
MEDIA
Cincinnati, Ohio

Book and cover design by Mark Sullivan
Cover image © Veer | Elena Chauvin

LIBRARY OF CONGRESS CATALOGING-IN-PUBLICATION DATA
Zielinski, Karen.
Hope and help for living with illness / Karen Zielinski.
pages cm.
ISBN 978-1-61636-468-7 (alk. paper)
1. Caregivers—Prayers and devotions. 2. Terminal care—Religious aspects—Christianity. 3. Sick—Prayers and devotions. 4. Suffering—Prayers and devotions. I. Title.
BV4910.9Z55 2012
248.8'61—dc23
2012030115

Published by Franciscan Media.
28 W. Liberty St.
Cincinnati, OH 45202
www.FranciscanMedia.org

Printed in the United States of America.
Printed on acid-free paper.
12 13 14 15 16   5 4 3 2 1

CONTENTS

It has always both surprised and disappointed me that a religion which has a crucified man as its central symbol still often has such a poor understanding and practice around issues of suffering and the healing of suffering. (I accept the common distinction that pain is the discomfort itself, and suffering is our attitude toward that pain or discomfort.) The world would think that we Christians would have a very redemptive and transformative understanding of human suffering and even cosmic "suffering."

This is especially true since this same Jesus, during his lifetime, made various forms of healing and the alleviation of suffering his primary ministry. Later forms of clerical ministry got themselves involved in "sin management" it seems; but for Jesus, the starting point was never sin, it was always suffering. He went where the suffering was, and when he left there was less suffering. It was in this context that his message was both learned and taught.

In the last ten years, I have discovered a whole new locus for theology and spirituality emerging in the Western world. It is from the fields of hospice work and bereavement ministries, much more than from the expected university and monastery settings as in the past. I am not meaning to be critical of universities and monasteries; we surely still need them. Yet this spirituality appears to be a very Franciscan "alternative orthodoxy", emphasizing central issues like death, embodiment, suffering, transformation, life after death, and the quality of life before and in the "nearing death experience" itself (which is really all of life!). About this new "theology" I would say what they said of Jesus: It "has authority, but not like the authority of the scribes" (Matthew 7:28). It is much more the authority of lives and hearts changed than dogmas believed.

We are realizing that we have largely medicalized what seem to be inherently spiritual events, especially birth itself and death itself. I have seen paintings and posters of medieval churches, where what first looked like the side altars, were in fact, cubicles for the sick and dying. Church and hospitals were one and the same! They had lovely but daring names like Hotel Dieu and "Home for the Incurables," which you still come across especially in Europe. Did they know something that we have lost? I suspect our secularism and materialism has lost the essential link that Jesus clearly recognized—and lived—between human suffering and the encounter with God. Our job is to re-link (re-ligio) these worlds, and that is what is happening in this book.

I am intentionally writing a very short foreword here to merely make these core points—and then to point you toward a life and a book that will prove the actual truth of what I have briefly tried to say.

I am honored and excited that a Franciscan sister, one of the family, is offering you a concrete and very compassionate example of the Gospel of suffering and healing in our time. This is indeed the Franciscan alternative orthodoxy that finds the Gospel where both Jesus and Francis always knew and told us it would be found—in the suffering of humanity—not at the "top" of things nearly as much as what appears to be the bottom. And it ends up being not the bottom at all. This is the great turnaround!

Sr. Karen is a living example of how transformation into God happens, for her and for all of us too. Read this book and be comforted—and find the power here to offer new and real comfort to others, and to our suffering world.

Richard Rohr, O.F.M.

Center for Action and Contemplation

Albuquerque, New Mexico

ACKNOWLEDGMENTS

The Sylvania Franciscan women, my religious sisters, have taught me about hope and help for living a Franciscan life. They are my teachers, mentors, and friends, as well as women of generosity and wisdom. I am grateful for their love and support. My family taught me generosity and giving back despite illness. Their stories are woven into my heart and this book. I am most grateful to my sister, Judy Zielinski, O.S.F., a member of both groups, who does not coddle me, but always challenges me with words like "Why not?" or, "I think you can!" She helped me shape this book.

As a Franciscan sister who has lived with multiple sclerosis (MS) since 1975, I have dealt with needles, side effects from medications, unreliable electric carts, and more. I have been excluded from homes, celebrations, and events by the attitudes of other people. I have learned to wait for handicapped parking spaces, test results, and insurance company approval for tests and medicines. I have seen my own parents and relatives become ill and die, and have cried with friends who were diagnosed with cancer.

Health problems touch all our lives: Everyone will be a patient someday. Besides competent doctors and promising new therapies, what can be the most healing to us is very simple: another person's compassion. Compassionate care involves the whole person—physical, emotional, social, and spiritual. This care is inherently a spiritual activity. Just holding the hand of a patient can be a sacred, spiritual act. Little things like listening to a patient's fears can offer much comfort. Words are not even necessary.

Medical advances have shifted the focus of medicine from a relational, caring model to a technical, cure-focused one. One of the best ways to cope with health challenges is through the gift of our faith, weaving spirituality through the fabric of our health. Whatever health issues we face, we have at our disposal healing, helpful resources to make our situation a little less overwhelming. Through my experiences with health problems, I hope to share some spiritual coping and comforting practices in this book.

Sometimes the best medicine doesn't come from the doctor.

CHAPTER ONE

Saying, "I Have a Disease"

When he entered Capernaum, a centurion came to him, appealing to him and saying, "Lord, my servant is lying at home paralyzed, in terrible distress." And he said to him, "I will come and cure him." The centurion answered, "Lord, I am not worthy to have you come under my roof; but only speak the word, and my servant will be healed. For I also am a man under authority, with soldiers under me; and I say to one, 'Go', and he goes, and to another, 'Come', and he comes, and to my slave, 'Do this', and the slave does it." When Jesus heard him, he was amazed and said to those who followed him, "Truly I tell you, in no one in Israel have I found such faith. I tell you, many will come from east and west and will eat with Abraham and Isaac and Jacob in the kingdom of heaven, while the heirs of the kingdom will be thrown into the outer darkness, where there will be weeping and gnashing of teeth." And to the centurion Jesus said, "Go; let it be done for you according to your faith." And the servant was healed in that hour.

—*Matthew 8:5–13*

My dear friend Carol had just been diagnosed with multiple sclerosis. We talked, cried, and prayed together for hours over the phone. I do not remember what prompted it, but I told her she needed to say, "I have MS." This might sound like a simple thing to do, but it is a significant thing to do. Carol was beginning the journey of dealing with a life-changing disease, and saying she had the disease would make her diagnosis definite for her. She could not say the words right away, but eventually she did.

At first, I could not understand why she could not say she had MS. It is not a life-threatening disease, but one that affects the quality of life. People live for years with it—it is not fatal. But as I thought about Carol, I gradually realized that for all of us, saying we have a disease or health condition is a profound spiritual event in our life. It means admitting you have an imperfect body, acknowledging an uncertain future depending on how your health has been throughout your life, and it represents concerns about your family's emotional and financial security.

Words create a powerful reality. When I first read an editor's comment about me in a short bio, "Karen is a freelance writer and frequent contributor to *St. Anthony Messenger*," I was pleased, and then thought, "I am a writer!" It did not matter that I had been contributing to many magazines every month for more than fifteen years. When I saw it written, it became a reality outside of me. It objectified a part of my life. Words create a reality, but there can be more to the story, more that underlies the words.

When we do not or cannot say the words about our health, I wonder if we are thinking that if we do not say we have a health problem then, somehow, we don't. It takes honesty to admit that our hearing might not be as good as it used to be, or that we do not have enough energy or stamina to do household tasks after work. We might not hear the evening news on television unless we have the volume turned up, yet we will not say that our hearing is less than it used to be. Our knees are painful and our balance makes us wobbly, but we would not admit to needing a cane for stability. When I deny that one of my symptoms is worsening, I might be too proud to say my body is getting weaker.

Some words are easy to say: "I won the lottery!" or, "I got a promotion," or, "My daughter just had a baby." Words that speak of positive events or good fortune are not a challenge to write about or share with others. We share good news countless times in phone calls, when we meet people, or in our annual Christmas card letter. We are proud and happy about our good news. We all like movies with happy endings. But life is not always like a movie with a happy ending. There are other stories and endings that are difficult to embrace and say.

Sometimes it is hard to find the right words to talk about our diabetes, chronic pain, or disability. Often, we feel a bit uncomfortable because we do not know how to talk about our cancer, our cousin who lives with autism, or friends with emotional disorders, and yet finding words to use is actually pretty simple to do. The bottom line is to use language that puts people first.

We need to use "people-first" language when referring to ourselves and others with health conditions. People-first language means we put the person first and the health challenge second. For example, we need to say, "a man who is blind" rather than a "blind man," and "a woman who uses a wheelchair" instead of "a wheelchair-bound woman." American author Mark Twain mused, "The difference between the right word and the almost-right word is the difference between the lightning and the lightning bug."

We need to remember that the person, not the disease, matters first. It is important to remember that we are God's creatures and, although not perfect, we are wonderful creatures. When we acknowledge that we have a disease, we are remembering that we are people and the disease is not us, but a part of our bodies. It helps to keep a safe boundary on our disease.

Saying that we have a disease is not an easy task. Saying, "I have Alzheimer's," or, "I have cancer," can release many emotions that we have been suppressing. We have trouble saying that a parent has dementia, saying sometimes, "They are just a little forgetful." By saying that we have a disease, we acknowledge its reality and therefore can begin to face it. Although it might be difficult to say that we have a medical condition, naming the disease can be therapeutic because we are admitting that we are sick. Naming it helps put us in control. When we name it truthfully, we have started a healing process.

Maybe the difficulty for us in saying we have a disease is that when we say words like, "I have diabetes," we are not only stating a fact about ourselves, but acknowledging a complex emotional ownership that comes with the disease. When a doctor writes down a patient's diagnosis, he or she might feel sad or discouraged for their patient, but the emotional barrel of mixed feelings is ours. The doctor, or even our friends, can write an e-mail or a letter telling someone about our health. They might feel shocked or saddened about our health, but ultimately, it is *our* truth, *our* disease, and *our* package of emotions—anger, frustration, fear—everything that comes with our diagnosis. There is a big difference between saying that a friend has a disease and saying that we have a disease.

When we say what is wrong with us, we state objectively our health condition. We feel vulnerable when we admit there is something going on with our health, that we are not perfect. We might not want to admit we are not the perfect picture of health because saying we are sick could make others think we are weak, or incapable of doing our jobs. There is an underlying layer of uncertainty when we name our disease—of our uncertain future—how this disease will play out with all the tests, doctor's appointments, procedures, and recoveries.

Bring Words to Prayer

A safe, intimate place to say the difficult words about our health problem is in our daily prayer. Our Creator God loves us unconditionally and is gentle and caring. Talking with God and saying, "I have cancer," can be a step to recovery. The reality of what is happening in our lives is put into perspective. Sharing our health concerns with God in prayer can be a nonthreatening way to put order in our lives. Remembering God's presence with us can be freeing. Tell God how you feel.

If we are not ready to say the words about our health, we can practice it alone with God. Choose a safe time and place. It might be in your living room, sitting on your favorite chair with a candle burning. Or it might be when you are sitting in a library or waiting in church. Try to say, "I have ...," naming the disease or condition. There might be tears or frustration or anger. But what a wonderful start! You are doing something by acknowledging what is going on in your life. When we say the difficult words, we are being honest. That can be a freeing feeling. Then we can go on and continue embracing our disease.

It might take us several times to say the words. We might cry or get frustrated and stop our session with God. That's OK. Emotions are tangled up in our prayers and life. We are being honest with our process of acknowledging our disease. We are trying, and that is a blessed space to be in. God is with us in this intimate process, in the messiness of life. Just be with our creator. Ask God to heal our hearts and bodies.

We need to make our needs known. The Gospels seldom portray Jesus as going around healing everyone in sight. Rather, the sick and the poor come to him. Only occasionally does Jesus cure someone with a critical need. Almost always, Jesus must be asked by those who seek to be cured. Those who sought healing had to say that they were sick, or take action such as the woman who was healed after touching Jesus's cloak (see Matthew 9:20–22).

Writing is another way to name a reality in our lives. Words have power whether we say them aloud or write them down. Often, when we write something down about our lives, it is cathartic. We get the pain out of our hearts. It is placed somewhere else for a while. The event is still there in our lives, but when we name the problem, disease, or even the good in our life, it can be healing. We have power or control over it. It does not go away, but we place it in a safe perspective and might even begin to feel a little order in our life.

Sometimes when we are at work, a colleague might ask us to send a report or to copy a file. Or we might be at church potluck and we ask a friend for a recipe for a wonderful dessert they brought. A common response in both cases is "e-mail me" or, "write down the recipe." There is something about writing something down that makes it definite. It makes it real, like a receipt from the store or a copy of our birth certificate or high school diploma.

Our society is driven by countless forms of written proof, from letters of recommendation for jobs, prescriptions from our doctors for a drug, or even proof of baptism in our church. These words represent a reality in life.

Journaling—writing down our own thoughts, prayers, feelings, can be a means of healing. When we go to a room or place we call our own and quiet down, we can journal and articulate feelings like fear, anxiety, or God's deep love for us. When we write this way, we can be completely honest with ourselves because journaling is for us. We need to jot down what surfaces—good and bittersweet things, or even our dreams of recovery. You cannot go wrong when you write down your feelings, emotions, life events, and so on.

Public words can be therapeutic, too. In many self-help support groups, such as Alcoholics Anonymous, we hear members acknowledging their diseases, "Hi, I'm Beth and I'm an alcoholic." That is all part of the process of recovering.

We need to ask our God to help us say we are sick. We must not give up, but must be steadfast in asking for divine help. It might not happen immediately for us, but we really have to trust. I always feel that when I persevere spiritually, all of a sudden my prayers are answered and then I remember that I had been asking God to bless me with faithfulness to my request. We must be gentle with ourselves in this process of finding our words. It does not have to happen right away, but it needs to happen.

One heart patient adds, "At one time I could not talk about what was happening to me; now people can't get me to be quiet! I found that talking helped in my healing process."

Say it. Write it down. Name and claim your disease. It can be healthy. I've seen it work for myself and for others.

> Strive by your thinking, as well as by your praying, to fulfill in your daily life what you say with your lips in church, and make the Holy Spirit who speaks through your lips be glad to dwell in your heart. Our words and our lips should be in agreement.[1]
>
> —*St. Caesarius of Arles*

To Consider
- What do you think is stopping you from saying that you have a disease or condition? What good might come from saying that you have this?
- If you cannot say the name of your disease, can you write it down?

Prayer
Creator God, maker of earth and my body, bless me with courage to address and face the new health challenges my

body is experiencing. I am overwhelmed at times when I try to comprehend how my body and life might be changing. Help me, my God, have the courage to say what is happening to my health. Give me the gift of honesty as I face this phase of my body. Teach me to start the process of fully embracing my health problems. If I know you are with me, I can go ahead. I am not alone. Bless me, my God.

CHAPTER TWO

Prayer for a Medical Test

Do not let your hearts be troubled. Believe in God, believe also in me.

—*John 14:1*

"I have to be at the doctor's office by 9:30," Willie told me with dread in her voice. My neighbor was preparing for her annual colonoscopy. The day before the test, she was at home, drinking the prescribed liquid. The following day, her test was over in a half hour; her doctor would get back with her test results.

It is only natural to become a little nervous when we are faced with something new or unfamiliar. Whether it's driving to a new office building or shopping center, to having to change the way we did something at work, we can get a little insecure, and frustrated. We might be nervous because of the change in a procedure we had done hundreds of times. We might want to practice the new process, until it becomes routine or second nature to us. Some of us might get anxious when our "regular" test technician does not perform the test on us that day.

A medical test can make us uneasy, too. We might face a test that we have never had before, and it might be a test that can bring discomfort or pain. If we have gone through the test, we might be anxious because we know our bodies do not like going through it. Perhaps the biggest reason we get overwhelmed or worked up before a medical test is fretting over why our doctor ordered us to take it in the first place. Maybe sitting in a medical scanner or x-ray machine is not what is scaring us. More likely, we are terrified of the possible results of the test.

After her test, Willie and I chatted about how good she felt now that it was over. We agreed that any medical test—blood work, scans, MRIs—can cause stress. We both know we need to be good stewards of our bodies, and that medical tests are a necessity. But we also agreed we felt relief when they are over.

Medical tests seem to have three parts that make us anxious: the time before the test, the test, and the time after the test. That sounds pretty basic, but there are three distinct sections, each with its own stresses.

When our doctor first orders a test, we place it on our calendar and then put it at the back of our mind. As the test date gets closer, we start to get anxious about the upcoming procedure. We spend energy being nervous about the unknown, about something yet to happen.

We try to control what we can: finding out where the test will take place, arranging for a ride, and doing any preparations. We might also take time to pray that God releases us from any anxiety that is welling up inside before the test.

On the test day, we sometimes feel a whole new wave of anxiety. We dread the beige tube of the MRI scan, or the needles, or the x-ray machines. The large machines can make us feel alienated and alone.

One practice that helps me get through a test is to continuously sing a verse or a line from a hymn in my head. The third verse of the hymn "Whatsoever You Do" by Willard F. Jabusch, is comforting, especially the line "When I was anxious, you calmed my fears."[2] I sometimes sing it dozens of times during a test. It calms me. Quickly, it seems, the test is over, I survive, and leave the test room.

By the time we visit our doctor for our test results, we are faced with other thoughts. The medical tests are finished, but now new fears rise up to replace the former fears. Will we need surgery? Chemo? Has our chronic condition worsened? Will our doctor order more tests?

Some people have no problems taking medical tests, but for the rest of us, there are ways to lessen our fears. The only way I can get through a medical test is by asking God to accompany me. I pray during every test. Sometimes I pray my favorite prayer, the Memorare, over and over again, almost like a mantra. I repeat it many times when I am going through a dreaded MRI. After the test I ask God to bless my body and to be with me whatever the outcome of the test. When I pray before, during, and after a test, I do not feel so alone. I feel powerful and in control.

The Unknown

Most of us like the comfort of familiar things—a favorite recliner in our living room where we can put our feet up and watch the news or our favorite television shows. Our homes are set up for our convenience. We decorate our homes with art or objects that have emotional meaning to us and are beautiful. They make us feel safe and happy. Knowing where our medicine is stored, where we keep our keys, or how we arrange our bathrooms or kitchens are part of our well-being and comfort. We can control our environment. We are in charge of it—we are masters of our living space.

So many times, after a medical test or minor surgery, we feel better when we can recuperate in our homes. Our safe, familiar home offers healing and spiritual comfort. We know where everything is, and even know all the sounds at our home: the creaks at night or the neighbor's dog barking at the mail carrier. We use our internal energy to relax and get better. But if we leave our homes for a place that is not so familiar, like a medical center or doctor's office, we might get anxious. We can lose control of both our home environment and our healthy bodies.

Leaving our home for the supermarket, church, or a social outing might cause a little stress in our lives if we do not know how to get to the event, whether there will be ample parking, and how long the event will be. But the unknown of undergoing a medical test is quite a bit more challenging.

Those on the medical staff understand this and do what they can to make us more comfortable. In today's medical centers, designers try to address patients' stress by decorating their waiting rooms and even offices with calming pastel colors, trendy furniture, soft carpeting, and framed art on the walls. But we are still on edge. Peaceful waiting rooms cannot fool us. Deep inside we know that these are all attempts to mask the uncertainty of the test to follow.

The waiting rooms can be beautiful, but they are not our space or homes. More than that, they represent something we are not comfortable with—the unknown. Maybe it is the first time we have to undergo a certain medical test that is the uncertainty. It can also be we are thinking about the unknown results the tests might discover. Another unknown can be the medical follow-up. Will we need more tests, new or different medical procedures, harsher medications, ongoing therapies? That possible medical future is what can cause the churning in our hearts.

While I wait in the doctor's office, I sometimes think of people who live in countries that engage in torture and unjust imprisonment. This may seem a stretch, but it occurs to me that, like waiting to speak with a doctor or to undergo a medical test, one of the most agonizing aspects of imprisonment is the prisoner waiting for the interrogation or seeing soldiers walk by their cell. Nothing is done, but the spiritual and psychological stress is exhausting.

I think of Jesus before his crucifixion and the agony in the garden. As I get older, this part of his life speaks to me of the human condition—that we all have to live with suffering, and that we are one with Jesus, who suffered. I find comfort in sharing my spiritual struggles with Jesus and solidarity in sharing my physical struggles with my sisters and brothers in pain.

One of the worst aspects of suffering is the loss of control over one's destiny, the sense of loss of self-reliance, and the need to depend on others. We need to step back a few paces and realize that much of the mental anguish we experience due to this comes from our previous intense desire (sometimes need) to establish our independence, our self-reliance, or from the perceived lack of support from others, even from God. We are not in the spiritual and psychological comfort of our own space. We all can remember our own medical agonies in the garden.

Letting Go

There comes a point in life when we might just have to really strip ourselves of our control over our bodies. We have to completely abandon our hearts and say, "Creator God, be with me now. I am frightened of all the unknowns that are unfolding. I have no power. I feel alone and vulnerable, but I have your companionship." That is enough. God is with us. What else can we do?

I remember sitting alone in a hospital waiting room after being called back for a second mammogram. Talk about agony. I received the phone call from the nurse when I got home on Friday after work at 5:30. In a recorded message, she told me that my mammogram needed to be done again—I could call the following Monday after 8 AM to reschedule or talk to a nurse! That weekend was torturous for me. It was the first time I ever had to retake a test. I was anxious, fearing the worst. I needed to get the test over as soon as I could.

The following week the technician took my second mammogram and told me to wait in the room in case another test needed to be taken. At some point in that room, my panic left me. I felt peace wash over me. I realized that I either had cancer or I did not, and there was nothing I could do about it. I could only do something about what the results were. I felt calm for the first time since that Friday answering machine message. I was not nervous any more. I had hope and trust that things would be all right. I truly was at peace.

My tests were normal. It seems that first tests were not clear, due to a technician's error. I was so grateful. Yet I also knew that, another time, I might receive challenging test results. I pray that I can take my accepting heart into that medical room for any future tests.

No matter what our position in life, our upbringing, or our wealth, we all share in the human condition. At some point in life, most people—doctors and bishops and children and movie stars—have to face a medical test. They lose control over their lives, if only for a short time. No matter how powerful or wealthy, they must face the unknown of a test, or a challenging prognosis. We all must face our tests—but how we approach the test can transform us.

Any day of the week, while talking with coworkers, at a lunch table with friends, or after a church service, someone might mention that a friend has to undergo a series of tests, a routine annual test, or a medical procedure. We share in their concern, and can offer them prayer and words that might lessen their anxiety. We have been there, and sharing our experiences could be our gift to their anxious soul. What a loving, healthy thing to do—to some way comfort a person facing a medical test. That is a win-win situation, with both people receiving a spiritual gift.

> If you have fear of some pain or suffering, you should examine whether there is anything you can do about it. If you can, there is no need to worry about it; if you cannot do anything, then there is also no need to worry. [3]
>
> —*Dalai Lama*

To Consider

- How do you prepare spiritually and emotionally for a medical test?
- Name your fears about having this test or procedure. Can you share your concerns about your fears and hesitancies with your doctor, nurse, or medical professional?

Prayer

Creator God, maker of earth and my body, bless me with health of mind and body as I face diagnostic tests, surgeries, and medical procedures. As I enter into the unknown area of finding out what might be wrong with me, I am anxious. I am powerless at these times, and I ask you to gently calm my heart and mind as I face these needles, scans, and blood tests. I ask you to be with me, to surround me with your love and peace as I face new and difficult health challenges. If I know you are with me, I can go ahead. I am not alone. Bless me, my God.

CHAPTER THREE

When Someone We Love Becomes Ill

But now thus says the LORD, he who created you, O Jacob, he who formed you, O Israel: Do not fear, for I have redeemed you; I have called you by name, you are mine. When you pass through the waters, I will be with you; and through the rivers, they shall not overwhelm you; when you walk through fire you shall not be burned, and the flame shall not consume you.

—Isaiah 43:1–2

John fell while taking his trash to the curb and broke his hip. He had surgery, followed by several weeks in a rehab facility, and finally returned home. Once there, he never seemed as healthy as he once was...he was weaker, and just not the same. His wife noticed this and was worried. Every time his children came to visit, they saw how diminished he had become.

Whether it's one of our parents who receives a diagnosis of dementia, an elderly aunt who needs to move to assisted living, or a dear friend who learns they have heart disease, the news is tough, traumatic—not only to the person diagnosed, but to their loved ones. Serious sickness is not only hard on the people who suffer with it, but also on the people who love them and must care for them. Those who are not sick can feel shocked, overwhelmed, and ultimately powerless.

Just like watching a child who is out of our reach and is about to fall down before our eyes, we feel helpless. We often wish that the fall or the tough diagnosis were ours. We do not want our child or loved one to be ill. When parents lose a child, they experience feelings of deep emotional loss and often remark, "Why my child? Why not me—I feel so helpless. I've lived my life!"

A serious diagnosis creates a bundle of strong emotions: shock, loss of control, grief, and anxiety about upcoming medical procedures, fear about the long-term prognosis, and worry over financial issues. We cannot see the long road that lies ahead. We feel a loss when we see our loved ones weaken, realizing they are no longer quite themselves, able to do what they could formerly do. Both the person with the declining health and their loved ones are experiencing the effects of the diagnosis. When we say things like, "I wish it were me," we are probably feeling like we could have a bit more control over the situation if it were in our hands alone. That is not true either: Disease causes a loss of control in all of us.

Dealing with the facts can help us feel like we have at least a little control over the disease. Finding the best specialists in town, a helpful support group, and state-of-the-art medical services for the patient at home or in medical venues can offer us hope. We seem to be doing something positive, we feel we are making progress, battling the disease, and taking action when we are addressing the medical part of a diagnosis. What can be far more challenging, though, is facing the emotional fallout.

Learning about the disease, talking to a host of doctors, surgeons, nurses, and so on, can be draining. Reading about the disease on the Internet, hearing about it on TV talk shows, talking to someone who's been through the journey them-selves—all this information can be unsettling and daunting. When we take a loved one for tests or conferences, we can both feel frightened. Having to make decisions—Should they choose chemo? Surgery? Neither? wears us out. Should they try a new medicine? An experimental procedure? A new doctor? What's the best option?

We have to make difficult life-and-death decisions and can feel confused and uncertain. We might feel angry with God, or we might not know why we are angry. Often we feel alone and helpless. A wave of wishing that we had the illness or disease instead of our loved one might sweep over us many times through the journey. We need to ask God to help us remember that he is with us, has always been with us and will stay with us. There is no way around—only through—but God is with us on the journey.

Being There

Your loved one is not only going through physical pain and discomfort at this time of illness, but emotional and spiritual pain, too. Our focus should be on them, on what we can do to make them feel better. Sometimes we can simply ask them, "What can I do that would make you feel better?" Most of us are taught not to ask for things, not to be burdens to others. But a person who is sick might just ask us to bring a book, to water their flowers at home, or to deliver some groceries to their house. These everyday things might offer them the sense that they are still smack in the middle of life, despite their medications, needles, and procedures. It can offer some normality to their medical whirlwind.

Healing the body is closely linked to healing the soul. When a person is ill, they are dependent because of their vulnerable condition. When we visit them, we need to remember to treat them with dignity and respect. We can ask them if they want to share what is going on in their illness or medical procedures, or talk about their fears, anger, or feelings of hopelessness. We are privileged to be there with them. This is active listening and sacred presence. When we invite people to share with us, they will say what is foremost on their mind. We do not have to be afraid that we are not trained chaplains or therapists.

Many patients like us to listen to them. They really appreciate a listening ear, even if we have heard their symptoms or fears before. The words of Scripture can offer us comfort in these difficult times.

Your family or friend might appreciate praying with you. We should not shy away from prayer or talking about God if our friend or loved one seems interested in prayer. We might offer a spiritual book or magazine, a meditation tape, or some recorded religious hymns or even a copy of the parish hymnal. Pray with your loved one, and remember the firm, comforting words from the prophet Isaiah in the song, "Be Not Afraid":

> Be not afraid.
> I go before you always.
> Come follow me, and
> I will give you rest.[4]

I often pray these words or sing them when I am waiting with someone who has to go through a medical procedure or is waiting for test results. I usually touch them, to reassure them that they are not alone. I might hold their hand or place my hand on their arm. Sometimes I even pray with a friend over the phone.

We need to speak with God repeatedly, reminding ourselves that we are not alone and seeking the strength to accept whatever is. This surrendering to God, for me, is the beginning of dealing with a serious health problem. We do not face these situations every day in our lives. They can be frightening. They call us to be vulnerable, trusting, and very honest. We may be frightened but we know that we are not alone.

Taking Some Control

Whether our loved one's illness is sudden or chronic, we can take some control of their health journey by taking care of ourselves. The illness is part of our lives, bringing chaos, urgency, and many questions we answer as we go along. Getting a diagnosis of a health crisis does not happen every day, but we need to be there for our loved ones, and we need to do that by taking care of ourselves, too.

I remember when one of my friends, a social worker, was facing a series of serious medical tests and possible surgery. I voiced my worry and fear about her upcoming ordeal and she told me to relax. She pointed out that I could not help her if I wasn't going to take care of myself. She then offered me six tips that she had taught her clients over the years:

1. *Get focused.* We need to eat properly, get enough rest, and some exercise, even if it is just walking around the hospital when we visit our loved ones. We must keep ourselves healthy during this difficult time.

2. *Get informed.* Knowledge is power, and the more we know about the disease, local resources, support groups, and our doctors, nurses, therapists, caregivers, and so on, the more we can navigate the experience.

3. *Get answers.* A big gift to your ailing loved one is you being an advocate for them, especially if they are not feeling well.

Noticing new symptoms or side-effects from medications or treatment options and telling the medical staff can be helpful. This can be a time to ask your loved one about their treatment preferences, where they might like to go if they need rehab, or what they want to do about their legal affairs. It might be awkward to ask, but your loved one might be relieved if you do.

4. *Get support.* With time spent in the medical world, we need to put our lives in perspective. We should stay involved in our school or work activities, connect with friends for a movie, dinner, or some activity we enjoy. This is not selfish. We really need to reach out to friends and family to stay connected. Friends and family can play a part on our wellness team.

5. *Get control.* This might sound impossible, but with so many things out of our control in this health challenge, we have to take little steps. We can determine the time we visit our loved one, and schedule an hour visit. When our mom is having an x-ray, we can get a cup of coffee and call a friend. When we help them make decisions, however small, like what to have for dinner, or what to wear, we can create a little normality in a chaotic experience.

6. *Hold on to hope.* When a serious diagnosis comes about, we probably waver between thinking the worst and hoping for a recovery. The fact is, we do not know how the future will unfold. This is a time for faith, for speaking with our pastor or dear friends.

What Do You Say?

Do not let the fact that you do not know what to say keep you away from spending time with your loved ones. You might simply tell them that you love them, or ask, "Do you want to talk about it?" Let them tell you what's on their mind. A good listener needs to be present and to wait. You can acknowledge their words, but let them speak; avoid the temptation to take over the conversation or finish their sentences.

If a person does not feel well that day and they are silent, that is fine. Silence might make us uncomfortable, but it is not about us—it is about how our friend feels. They do not need anything but our presence some days. If you can accompany a loved one to a medical test, doctor's appointment, or medical treatment, your presence is a warm gift in contrast to all the cold, impersonal machines and equipment. The healing in our presence to those in need flows from God's presence to us.

Sickness is a part of life. Although we cannot cure every disease, what we can offer our ailing loved ones is our presence. Talk to them. If you live out of town, call them, and listen. Offer your prayers and love and be with them in true support. Do not worry about saying the right words. Let them know you care. That is a sacred gift.

Dealing with a sick person whom we love dearly can be very difficult. We need to give them time, listening, and patience. We can offer strong doses of compassion, empathy, and caring— exactly what Jesus, the great healer, offers us. One chaplain I

know offered some simple words to say out loud: I'm sorry.
I want to help if I can. You're a wonderful friend. I love you.

The Lord Jesus, who went about doing good works
and healing sickness and infirmity of every kind,
commanded his disciples to care for the sick, to pray
for them, and to lay hands on them. In this celebration
we shall entrust our sick brothers and sisters to the
care of the Lord, asking that he will enable them to
bear their pain and suffering in the knowledge that, if
they accept their share in the pain of his own passion,
they will also share in its power to give comfort and
strength.[5]

—*The Pastoral Care of the Sick*

To Consider

- Can you talk with your loved one about their concerns?
  Pain? Loss of body functions? Being a burden to others?
- Even if you cannot talk with the other person, offer to pray
  with them, or just visit and let them talk about whatever
  they want to talk about.

Prayer

Creator God, maker of earth and our bodies, bless us with
health of mind and body as my loved one faces sickness. I feel
helpless and unable to say "the right words" at this dark time.
We are overwhelmed. I ask you to help me to say the words
that might support and comfort them. I offer most of all, my

simple presence with them, to simply be with them, as they face serious health problems. I ask you to be with us as we together come to terms with this illness. I know you are with us and we trust we will be all right. We are not alone. Bless us, O steadfast God.

CHAPTER FOUR

Caring for the Caregivers

And the king will answer them, "Truly I tell you, just as
you did it to one of the least of these who are members
of my family, you did it to me."

—*Matthew 25:40*

I'm not the only one living with multiple sclerosis.

My sister Judy is, too, when she picks up some groceries for
me when she visits me from South Bend. So is my neighbor
Carol, who gathers my mail and leaves it outside my door.
When my Franciscan sisters Rosalma and Maria share a home-
made meal with me or help me unload groceries from the back
of my van, or when my friends Sue and Joanne bring lunch to
work or my home when the weather is cold and rainy and they
don't want me venturing outdoors—they, too, are living with
MS.

When someone gets ill, many others are affected as well.
No one lives with a disease in a social (or spiritual) vacuum.

Family, friends, and neighbors often rally around those with chronic or mental illness, and help according to their gifts. They are following the Gospel mandate to help their neighbor. A caregiver is a gift to those who receive their generous, loving help. Sometimes, just calling someone who is ill or praying with them is a huge help.

Caregivers come in all ages and help in a variety of ways, doing whatever needs to be done. They cross boundaries of age, faith, ability, and services rendered.

My mother was a caregiver to me when I visited her at her home in Detroit. After teaching high school all week, I would drive to Detroit on Friday after school. I remember sitting in the living room, putting my feet up on the recliner, and my eighty-five-year old mother would bring me a cup of tea or a snack. I felt embarrassed, humbled, and powerless. I told my mom how I felt, and she said it was "no big deal." But it was a very big deal to me. She was my caregiver and the fact that she was at an advanced age did not matter to her.

Some people with health problems might claim they do not have any caregivers but they probably have several of them. Most family and friends are specialized caregivers. Our brothers or sisters might drive us to medical appointments while our neighbors pick up milk and bread at the grocery store. Sometimes nephews or nieces take out the trash, climb ladders to change light bulbs, or do light cleaning. Another might sort out insurance forms, pay medical bills, or call the doctor's office for clarification on prescriptions or upcoming medical procedures.

A caregiver might make a weekly visit to a sick friend or relative. My brother Jim always stopped in to see my mother on Mondays after work. He did odds and ends like taking out the recyclables or carrying some canned goods from her basement pantry. Mom would then cook a meal so that Jim could sit down and share some delicious food with her. It was a win-win situation.

Some caregivers help with medical procedures: changing bandages, administering eye drops, or giving injections. Others might bring us a pot of soup, a DVD, or just stop by to visit. When we are sick, our health status can vary from day to day—from weather-related pain to the side-effects of chemo and some caregivers simply stop by to check up on the patient. They might ask if they feel well enough for company that day, or if they need anything. Caregivers offer a variety of gifts, and they should focus on their own interests and strengths if they can. If a caregiver likes to drive they might help with transportation to medical appointments or to the grocery store or shopping mall. Some caregivers might like to help with correspondence, paying bills, or computer work.

Offering loving service to someone who is ill is a profound component of our Christian value of service. Caregiving shows the faithfulness that love brings. Giving time to help the sick offers both the caregiver and the one receiving the care an opportunity to think of and be grateful for the other. In this, I am reminded of marriage vows: "For better or for worse, in sickness and in health...." That is the deep love also found in caregiving.

Caregivers are prone to burnout. Caring for the chronically ill can bring a change in family dynamics that can disrupt households and put a burden on finances. The lives of everyone concerned are changed, and both those who are giving care and those who are receiving care can feel powerlessness, irritability, isolation, despair, and resentment. It is only human to have these types of reactions.

Ongoing communication with the person receiving care is critical. Besides talking about their medical care, patients need to voice their feelings. They must be able to voice their spiritual and emotional needs along with their physical needs. We should encourage them to take an active role in their caregiving. This may seem basic, but often we caregivers do too much for those we are helping. As caregivers, we need to ask them if they want to or can do a few tasks themselves—folding laundry, making a simple meal, watering plants, and the like.

When we talk to them, we need to give them the power and permission to be in control of their lives as much as possible, and allow them to be as independent as they possibly can. This applies to both their physical and emotional needs. We can check with their doctor to see if it is safe for them to do a few simple tasks: get up occasionally to get a plate, turn on the dishwasher, or organize some mail or items in a closet or pantry. Movement can help with their independence and can often fend off physical complications due to inactivity.

Most of all, we need to remember that although a person is sick, they are still human and we must respect their dignity. Ask the person what they need with regard to dressing, bathing, or eating. It can help to think of how we ourselves would want to be treated in a particular situation.

If we treat those for whom we are caring with respect and dignity, we can help them avoid feelings of humiliation and frustration. If they do a small task well, we can encourage them and tell them how we see their growth, their improvement from the last time we visited them. Being loving and gentle with our patient is truly living out the corporal work of mercy, to visit the sick.

Just Say, "Thank You Very Much"

Whether you are a caregiver or a person who needs a caregiver, you are in a challenging part of your life. Caregiving is a two-way street. Although illness might bring on a depressed mood, self-absorption, and fear, the person receiving the care still needs to offer thanks to the caregiver. It's important to give back however you are able. A simple phone call, a hug, or just saying, "Thanks, I appreciate all you do for me," goes a long way. A written note, a flower, or a candy bar given to a faithful caregiver can be a touching gift. Everyone needs to be affirmed and loved.

A helpful practice is to imagine ourselves in the opposite role. If you are a patient, think of how you would feel if you were a caregiver. You visit a person who is sick. You drive to see them, perhaps after working at a hectic, stress-filled job. Then you fight bad weather or rush-hour traffic to get to your loved one's home. The loved one is not feeling well and might be a bit cranky if you are late. The caregiver is both emotionally and physically tired, too. Acknowledging the caregiver is a matter of graciousness and gratitude. It is healthy for both—the person who is ill steps out beyond self-absorption, and the caregiver is affirmed for their personal outreach, both emotional and physical. It might be helpful to remember that neither the caregiver nor the patient wants to be in this place.

Caregivers should think about how they would feel if they were the one needing help, unable to write a check, cook a meal, or do a load of laundry because of weakness or medical side-effects. As a patient who might not drive any more, or who cannot walk well, climb stairs, or do many of the simple tasks of everyday living, they are feeling losses in many areas of their lives. When we retire and no longer work, we try to deal with how we can use our new free time. But when the free time comes unexpectedly or unplanned, we can perhaps feel a great loss of integrity, isolation, dignity, and even self-worth.

The task for a caregiver is immense. While juggling their own jobs and family responsibilities, caregivers can feel overwhelmed by their added role. They might try to compensate for the added caregiving tasks by dropping out of their own lives: commitments like attending their children's sporting events or school activities, going to movies or dinner with friends, or even church services. Sometimes caregivers turn to escapist behaviors to cope with their feelings of cynicism or being trapped. They might turn to drinking, drugs, or shopping binges to cope with their negative feelings and resentment.

Caregivers might start these negative behaviors gradually and they might not even know that they are involved in them. A good friend might be wise to tell them. Sometimes a friend, family member, or a health care professional can help a caregiver become aware of potentially destructive behavior that results from feelings of frustration and inadequacy on the caregiver's part. Friends might direct them to a counselor, or to other church or community resources that can help manage a variety of needs: financial help, delivered meals, daily planning, nursing visits, and pastoral programs.

Perhaps the most profound yet simple way to sensitively understand the nature of the caregiver and patient roles is the fact that both are people-first roles. These roles involve a give and take of both parties having spiritual, physical, emotional, and social needs that change dramatically due to a diminishment of one's health. They are partners in a place that we do not willingly visit—the somber dependence that illness can bring, either for a short time or for the rest of one's life.

A good spiritual resource might be found in area caregiver groups. Many libraries, churches, non-profit organizations, and hospitals offer sessions that address the many challenges caregivers face. These can be helpful and offer real life experiences from those who have experience in the ministry of caregiving. Sometimes attending these sessions can offer new insight or ways to work with your loved one that are most helpful in day-to-day care. You can also look for social groups or prayer groups where caregivers can go for a cup of coffee, soup, or just an opportunity to sit with others who understand what they are experiencing.

We need to acknowledge our faithful caregivers. Collectively, their ministry affects the health of thousands. If you have difficulty writing a thank-you note, or getting a card or flower for your caregiver, try this: Show your caregiver this chapter in this book. They will know you love them and are grateful. So thanks, Judy, Willie, and Carol, Rosalma and Maria, Sue and Joanne, and everyone who cares for me!

> Blessed are those who love the others when they are sick and unable to serve, as much as when they are healthy and of service to them. Whether in sickness or in health, they should only want what God wishes for them. For all that happens to them let them give thanks to our Creator.[6]
>
> —*St. Francis of Assisi*

To Consider

- *For the patient*: How do you feel towards the people who care for you? Are you able to communicate your needs and wants with them? Have you thanked them recently?
- *For the caregiver*: Have you ever experienced burnout in your role as a caregiver? What are some of the most challenging feelings you have had in this type of relationship? Anger? Jealousy? Misunderstanding?

Prayer

Creator God, maker of earth and my body, bless me with the gifts I need as I enter this sacred ministry called caregiving. I am happy to give service to my loved one, but I am unsure of the future. Will I be a good, kind caregiver? I do not know if I have the stamina to faithfully keep this up. Sometimes I am overwhelmed. I ask you to gently calm my heart and mind as I face this challenging test of love. Embrace us both with your strength and peace as we live each unfolding day. I know you are with me. I am filled with hope as I cling to you. I am not alone. Bless me, my God.

CHAPTER FIVE

Anxiety About Health Insurance

And now, my daughter, do not be afraid, I will do for you all that you ask, for all the assembly of my people know that you are a worthy woman.

—Ruth 3:11

"How sick should I let myself get before I go to the doctor? I just lost my health insurance." My friend Mary was devastated by her recent diagnosis, which was complicated by the fact that she did not have health coverage. It was a double blow: to be diagnosed with a disease and then not have insurance to cover the treatments.

Mary has a complicated history of heart disease. For the last three years, this college graduate and mother of two grown sons has endured several stress tests and heart catheterizations, had five stents and a pacemaker implanted, and lived through a botched coronary artery dissection. Her body rejected the stents, and she spent over $250,000 on more coronary tests as doctors tried to diagnose her heart problems.

For seventeen years, Mary had been a nationally licensed loan originator and branch manager for a mortgage company, earning almost $100,000 a year. She worked completely on commission and relied on her executive husband's excellent medical insurance coverage.

Things changed for Mary when her husband left her and they divorced. She lost her job in the struggling economy, losing her health insurance after COBRA ran out. (COBRA stands for the Consolidated Omnibus Budget Reconciliation Act of 1985, which allows employees to keep their health insurance for up to eighteen months when they lose their jobs.)

Time passed, and Mary was left with little health coverage. Not only did she have an uncertain future of heart disease at a relatively young age, but she also had the added stress and burden that, without a health insurance plan, she could not get the medical care she needed. She wondered if there were medical procedures or medications that would help her get healthier, then obsessed about how she could pay for them. What if there was, and she could not get it because she could not afford it?

For many people, the struggle with rising healthcare costs has already reached a critical point. In 2011, more than two in five American adults under age sixty-five had trouble paying their medical bills, according to a study by the Commonwealth Fund, a New York–based health policy research group. Of those people, 39 percent had used up all their savings, 30 percent had racked up huge credit card debt to pay their medical bills, and 29 percent said medical bills left them struggling to pay for basic necessities such as food and heat.

The fact is that thousands of people have medical conditions that need attention but they have no health insurance. Thousands of people have no medical insurance to cover preventive healthcare. So people are getting sick and have no way to take care of their health.

Even if people are employed with healthcare benefits, these costs are rising exponentially. Co-pays and deductible rates are rising. My health insurance carrier was the same for three years. When I ordered an injectable drug for my multiples sclerosis, I found it had doubled in price! I was shocked!

Health Care Choices

At any given moment, people are losing their jobs. Three industries alone—manufacturing, construction, and professional and business services—account for nearly three-quarters of total jobs lost in the stressed economy. Besides losing their paycheck, they face a loss of health benefits. Sometimes those benefits affect the entire family, children and their checkups, inoculations, tests for playing school sports. The loss of health insurance is monumental in a person's life. Parents are especially overwhelmed with worry about the health and wellness of their children and family members.

It seems that no one is untouched by loss of heath care benefits. People of all ages and areas of work—executives, teachers, direct service, skilled, and unskilled workers— can lose their jobs in a heartbeat. Not only are wages gone, but so is health care for employees and their families. People are forced to make tough choices about how they will take care of their medical bills. Sometimes families cannot afford food or gasoline because of health bills.

If a family is young and relatively healthy, they might hope that they stay healthy and skip going to their doctors or dentists. They might get by without medical care because of their youth. That might work for a while, but the whole attitude of wellness, healthy prevention, or taking good care of our bodies to prevent future serious and costly procedures cannot be practiced when there is no health insurance.

Sometimes families have to rely on the kindness of strangers. Schools, local libraries, civic centers, hospitals, and colleges often offer health fairs. Some area dentists offer free dental cleanings and even dental work free of charge. Other health events offer free blood pressures readings, blood tests, diabetic supplies, free bandages, and information about medications and other free clinics.

Getting healthcare from these free health fairs can be humbling to us, we who were independent, who worked at a good-paying job until, through no fault of our own, the job ended. We feel embarrassed and vulnerable. Why should we check the paper for free medical fairs or clinics? Yet we need to investigate any local health events in our area because we owe it to ourselves and our families. We must be good stewards of our bodies, created by our God.

Since the start of the 2008 recession, millions of workers have lost the health coverage that their jobs provided, based on data from the U.S. Census Bureau and the Bureau of Labor Statistics. Approximately one million of these losses occurred monthly, which amounts to thousands of workers a day.

Although we might be humbled to seek healthcare from a variety of resources, the nurses and healthcare professionals at these clinics are sensitive to our needs. They want to help and they can. Why not let others who understand people's health insurance plight help us? We need to stay healthy during this awkward time of transition in our economy. God is calling us to true humility at these times.

For general health care and dental health, local healthcare events might be all a family needs. But what happens when there is a life-threatening diagnosis? My friend Barb was diagnosed with cancer. Her family physician directed her to an oncologist who saw her at a very low cost and waived many of his fees. Barb's treatment plan called for radiation and medication. She talked with her doctor and he made a treatment plan for her recovery.

So what do you do when you need medical help and have no money or health plan? Some people acknowledge their vulnerability and ask for help. To do this we may need to swallow our pride, but it is a true Christian and human response. We ask when we need help and cannot do it on our own. We call on our community of friends, church members, and family. Asking for help might seem like a last resort, or feel like begging. But it is a start on our sacred journey to a solution of how to fix our health. We need each other. When we do not know what else we can do, we can ask for all kinds of support from others.

The first Barb did was to gather her family and some friends. She wanted to inform them about the status of her cancer and the challenges of her medical costs. She told them that if they wanted to give her any gifts for Christmas, her birthday, or any other special occasion, she would appreciate help with paying for her medications. Although it was a difficult thing for Barb to do, the response was a blessing. Family and friends rallied behind her.

One relative got on the computer and investigated several pharmaceutical companies who manufactured Barb's medication. Many of the companies have scholarships and give free medication for those in need. Others knew friends who had just gone through a similar health crisis, and called to see it they knew about any other resources or programs that helped patients with transportation and other needs. Still others in the group offered to call a few nurses in the area to see if there were any other programs that could help in Barb's situation.

Barb received several monetary gifts after that gathering with her family, but her biggest gift was the understanding, guidance, tears, prayers, and simple presence of her loved ones.

It was their assurance that they would be there for here. Her family assured her that, "It takes a village, and we are your village."

Emotions Are Fragile

In her struggle with heart disease and lack of insurance, Mary repeatedly prays for courage and is inspired by St Paul's word to the Ephesians: "Finally, be strong in the Lord and in the strength of his power. Put on the whole armor of God, so that you may be able to stand against the wiles of the devil" (6:10–11). She prays these words over and over, trying to be strong during her times of challenge and adversity. "Without my faith, I would have given up," Mary reflects, "I believe God has a reason for me to be here today."

Mary believes that she has to take control of her health and be proactive. She has researched other health insurance policies, but getting coverage is a challenge because of her pre-existing condition. She found some "coupon policies," which gave coupons that take some of the cost off procedures. She looked into her state's mandated coverage plan, but it was expensive and only allowed a very limited number of annual doctor visits. She was finally approved for permanent disability, but since she did not have a terminal condition, her state did not place her on Medicaid. "I feel like I am walking on eggs right now; I could be bankrupt in two days. My pacemaker cost me $50,000!" Mary says. "I dread thinking about the high cost of my prescription drugs."

Losing control of her healthcare independence is humbling for her. She is trying to find a part-time job, but knows she might have to rely on her family, her church, or social agencies to carry her through tough times. Until Mary gets placed on Medicaid, she clings to hope and embraces good health practices along with wellness and prevention techniques.

The truth is that we are all a hairbreadth away from health tragedies—serious illness, death of a loved one, financial ruin, estrangement from our spouse, children, parents, or friends. We are not in control of anything. The answer is to recognize this and to realize that God is our refuge, our strength, our rock. Jesus is right here in our midst. Never alone, we can walk with him.

> Character cannot be developed in ease and quiet. Only through experience of trial and suffering can the soul be strengthened, vision cleared, ambition inspired, and success achieved.[7]
>
> —*Helen Keller*

To Consider

- If you currently have medical insurance, have you made any plans to pay for future medical expenses if your insurance coverage stops for some reason?
- What wellness practices and prevention techniques are you currently using? Are there other practices you can begin in order to be as healthy as possible?

Prayer

Creator God, maker of earth and our bodies, bless us with health of mind and body during this time of illness, loss of health insurance, and the uncertain future. Not only is our health changing, but the resources of taking care of it is, too. We feel dismayed and vulnerable. We do not know what to do or where to go for help. May we have hope during this frightening time. We ask for guidance that we might reach out to others for their wisdom. We know you are with us and we trust that all will be all right. We are not alone. Bless us, O steadfast God.

CHAPTER SIX

The Comfort of Prayer

Are any among you suffering? They should pray. Are any cheerful? They should sing songs of praise.

—*James 5:13*

I take care of my health: I visit my doctors, take my pills, and look after my well-being. Most importantly, I spend time in daily prayer because I know this is just as vital for my health as any medical procedure.

Praying for our health should be a part of all our healthy habits. People know what they should and should not eat to take care of their bodies; they know which pills they have to take to control their blood pressure or cholesterol; and they basically know what to do to stay healthy. Wellness information comes at us from many places: television news reports, books and magazines articles, opinions and ideas of our friends and families, and information we are given at our doctor's offices. Yet what we might not hear about very often is the integral part prayer holds in our health.

Creating a Sacred Space

I usually pray in a small "sacred space" that I have set up in the corner of my bedroom. It is my little refuge, a special place for prayer and healing. It is not necessary to have a separate room to pray—any corner in the house or even an uncluttered closet will do.

As we were growing up, my Dad prayed in our finished basement on his recliner. He had a list of intentions that he kept on a table next to his chair as he said his prayers and rosaries. When he died, I took this little note of prayer intentions and placed it on the table next to my chair. I also have my mother's prayer book there. These items help and comfort me as I pray and talk to my parents each day.

Next to my comfortable chair is my grandmother's table, which my dad refinished. On it is a scented candle, a cedar statue of St. Francis of Assisi, an old army photo of my dad, my mom's prayer book, and a rock from a pilgrimage that I made to Assisi, Italy. Under the table is a basket that holds my Office book, other books for spiritual reflection, a pen, and a journal. I keep some Band-Aids and a prescription bottle there as well, to remind me of my personal health and life story.

My prayer begins like this: I say a prayer to God the Creator, Jesus, and the Holy Spirit. I say the Memorare, addressed to the Blessed Mother, then speak with my deceased parents, relatives, sisters, and friends. I pray the Office, which is the traditional daily prayer of the Church and includes psalms, prayers, and readings from Scripture. Then I stop and sit in silence, without reading anything, just focusing on what I have just prayed. Finally, I read and reflect on the lectionary readings for that day.

Many times, I find myself distracted and try to get back on track. Sometimes I have to fight sleep; more often, I get distracted by what I have to do at work or by my health issues. An upcoming doctor's appointment or a medical test can weigh on my mind and make me anxious. At times like that I use my favorite Scripture quote, from John 14:13–14: "I will do whatever you ask in my name, so that the Father may be glorified in the Son. If in my name you ask me for anything, I will do it."

I take a deep breath, calm myself down a bit, and ask my Creator to be present to me during these times of distress. I ask for the gift of peace in my heart and in my mind. I focus on calming myself down. I ask, and I ask, and I ask. I get distracted so many times, but I somehow come back and ask my loving God to hear my needs, to soothe my troubled, worried heart.

Then it's time to go to work, and my prayer must end. Sometimes I wonder if I have even prayed, if anything has come of my time with my God? I reach for my coffee and finish it, utter a prayer of thanks, and leave my prayer space.

A few hours later, during the busy workday, I feel a sense of peace. I am amazed—my prayer has been answered. I cannot believe it! I still have my problems, but I now have a deep sense of well-being. I feel better about everything: all will be well. It dawns on me that my prayer for understanding and peace has been answered. I still have the health issues, and the people for whom I have been praying still have theirs. But I now feel like I can face these burdens; it was my prayer time that changed me. I was changed because I asked God to change my restless heart, and my prayer was answered.

Answers to prayer do not always happen within my timeline. I am usually impatient when I pray, and want my petitions or requests answered soon, if not immediately. But I have learned this is not the way it works. I believe that God always answers my prayers, but it may be days, months, or perhaps even years later that my prayer is answered. I consider this a spiritual timeline.

I ask God to heal me each day—from my human weaknesses, my lack of generosity, and other things I need to change to make me a more compassionate person. I also ask God to heal me of my multiple sclerosis, to help me be a better steward of my body by helping me lose weight and walk better.

I have prayed these requests daily for so long that it can be a surprise when an answer comes. For example, one day, out of the blue, I received a card from a friend who had moved out of my life. She was back in the area and asked me to meet her for lunch. We did, and through her that day God answered my request to walk better. This woman had been my first physical therapist, and now I asked her to give me a simple physical therapy program that would strengthen my legs. She did, and my walking has improved considerably.

Since 1975, the year I was diagnosed with multiple sclerosis, I have asked God, in Jesus's name, to heal me, to cure me of my MS. I believe God granted me this request because I am doing pretty well. New MS medications are being released frequently, and I have come to accept this devastating disease.

What is important in prayer is faithfulness—we need to do it regularly. Prayer is a ritual, a part of life that has a sacred pattern repeated over and over again. This ritual brings the sacred into our lives. Our rich faith tradition brings prayers, sacred words, and gestures that bring peace and meaning into our lives. We create a meaningful ritual when we pray for all good things, like our health.

I do not know if my theology of praying for healing is correct, but I do know that I cannot be wrong if I talk to God and ask for healing. Some people ask if my prayer for healing works. I believe it does. I feel that what God has allowed me to do in my life has been a gift. I have traveled to Assisi, Italy, and made a pilgrimage using my electric cart. Conventional wisdom would say, "Stay home." I prayed for safety, and God was with me in countless ways for three weeks. I prayed that I would lead a "normal" life and, looking back, I realize God has indeed answered my prayers.

I pray for a cure for MS. For over thirty years I have helped raise funds for research to end the effects of this devastating neurological disease. Years ago, I met the founder of the MS

Society, then gave a eulogy at her memorial service. I know we are close to a cure for this disease. It might not be in ten years, or on my timeline, but today there are medications that slow its progression. I know people in MS research who feel they are close to a cure, that it will happen in my lifetime, and I have to believe that prayer is a part of this progress.

Each day when I leave my prayer space and go to work, I still have to face the challenges of the day, but I am different, more peaceful. At night, I am drawn to my space again, light my candle, and pray my evening prayers. I sing a verse the chorus from the song "You Are Mine," by David Haas:

> I am strength for all the despairing,
> healing for the ones who dwell in shame.
> All the blind will see, the lame shall all run free,
> and all will know my name.
> Do not be afraid, I am with you.
> I have called you each by name.
> Come and follow me, I will bring you home;
> I love you and you are mine.[8]

Throughout the Old Testament we find God speaking to Moses or Samuel or Ruth or the Hebrews, telling them not to be afraid, to remember God is with them and that things will work out. These words stand for us today, too.

We are all called to prayer, to talk to our God about what is happening in our lives. When we are worried about health issues, who better to talk with? If a misunderstanding or quarrel takes place in our lives, we talk to the person involved in the situation. When we talk to the person and ask for clarification or forgiveness, we usually feel better and can begin healing. Placing our health concerns before our loving God must be a part of our total health care—right up there with doctor's visits and our medicines. Prayer is just what the doctor should order.

> Part of the plan laid out by God's providence is that we should fight strenuously against all sickness and carefully seek the blessings of good health, so that we may fulfill our role in human society and in the Church. Yet we should always be prepared to fill up what is lacking in Christ's sufferings for the salvation of the world as we look forward to creation's being set free in the glory of the children of God.[9]
>
> —*Pastoral Care of the Sick*

To Consider

- Do you have a special place set up for prayer? Do you spend quiet time praying, talking to God about how you are feeling?
- Do you ever talk to your doctor about prayer and your health?

Prayer

Creator God, maker of earth and our bodies, bless my imperfect, yet wonderful body. I know it is not perfect, but know you created me. I am concerned about the future, about my health and feel devastated about my illness. Help me to be faithful to prayer with you each day. You are my comfort and safe place. I trust you and ask that I will be all right. I will not be afraid. I know you will answer my prayer. Bless me, O my wonderful, comforting God.

CHAPTER SEVEN

Living With Mental Illness

I waited patiently for the LORD;
   he inclined to me and heard my cry.
He drew me up from the desolate pit,
   out of the miry bog,
and set my feet upon a rock,
   making my steps secure.
He put a new song in my mouth,
   a song of praise to our God.
Many will see and fear,
   and put their trust in the LORD.

—Psalm 40:1–3

"I knew as a mother that there was something wrong with Jenny," said Eve. (Names have been changed to protect people's privacy.) Eve and her husband had adopted Jenny, who was an extremely active child. When she reached puberty, Jenny's behavior became troublesome and unusual. Eve, a nurse, looked to various medical professionals for a diagnosis and a psychiatrist finally, but hesitantly, diagnosed Jenny with bipolar disorder.

According to the National Library of Medicine, bipolar disorder is a condition in which people go back and forth between periods of being in a very good mood, and being in a very irritable mood or in depression. The swings between mania and depression can be very quick. Bipolar disorder affects men and women equally, and usually begins between the ages of fifteen and twenty-five. The exact cause is unknown, but it occurs more often in relatives of people who also have bipolar disorder.

When Jenny was first diagnosed in the mid-1980s, there were not many treatments or medications for the disorder. And so at sixteen, she was put on lithium. Taking this medication was a real challenge for a high school student who was active, quick-witted, and bright; it frustrated Jenny, since it slowed her down to a more "normal" pace, something she was not used to.

Even on the medication, Jenny's behavior was disturbing. She was promiscuous, spent money recklessly, and once took an airline trip to Chicago after telling her parents she was staying at a friend's house. Jenny displayed the classic symptoms of bipolar disorder: she was easily distracted, had little need for sleep, showed poor judgment and temper control, behaved recklessly, and lacked self-control.

Jenny had many car accidents because she used poor judgment

when driving. She wasn't consistent in taking her medicine, especially on weekends, because it made her feel groggy and confused. Life was a challenge for Jenny and her family.

After high school, Jenny moved to California, married, and had a son. Then at twenty-five, she committed suicide. After her death, Eve discovered that her daughter had signed all the medical release forms and legal papers so Eve could care for her three-year-old grandson. During this time of grief, Psalm 34:18 offered Eve some comfort: "The LORD is near to the brokenhearted, and saves the crushed in spirit." Eve traveled to California and brought Jimmy, her young grandson, to her home to live with her.

Eve and her husband adopted Jimmy. Eventually, they discovered that Jimmy, too, had bipolar disorder, along with Attention Deficit Hyperactive Disorder (ADHD).

If he took his medicine, Jimmy was able to function in a relatively normal manner. He took a few courses at a vocational high school and was respectful to people in charge, but he was bullied at the school because he was different. At one point, Jimmy could not take the bullying any longer and got involved in a fight with the bully. He was arrested, went to court, served time in jail, and was suspended from school. There were no other options for Jimmy to continue his education, so he did not finish high school.

After her daughter's death and the experiences of her grandson, Eve is determined to educate people about mental illness. She says, "I am all for telling Jenny's story if it will help someone with mental illness. We first need to accept people where they are at, and once we do, they can rise to their potential and fulfill what God intends them to be." Eve tells that on a recent visit with Jimmy, he commented that, although his life was full of some tough challenges, "God saved me to do something special."

Mental Illness Is a Physical Illness

According to the National Institute of Mental Health, about 16–20 percent of the population has mental illness. Mental illness can occur at any age, and learning may or may not be affected. It has little to do with intellect: the IQs of people with mental illness may be normal or above average. Mental illness can be an acute or a chronic illness. It can vacillate between rational and irrational behavior. Sometimes mental illness may be accompanied by an intellectual disability or a physical disability. Normally, these diseases are treated by health care professionals with medication, psychotherapy, and counseling. Persons with mental illness do particularly well when supported by a circle of family, friends, and a faith community.

When someone is diagnosed with cancer or heart disease, we offer our concern and prayers for them and accept it as a reality of life. We feel comfortable talking about it and might ask for support and prayers. Yet mental illness is a legitimate disease, as well. It can be frustrating when people attach a negative, shameful stigma to people who have a mental illness, even though this stigma goes back centuries and includes the times when those who had mental illnesses were mistreated in hospitals and prisons. As Franciscan Fr. Richard Rohr wisely reflects, however, "God is not threatened by differences. It's we who are."

Mental illness brings along with it negative stereotypes and stigmas. Sometimes, even health care professionals can have a stigma against mental illness. They might tell their patients to stick to their medications and they will be all right. But it is a more complex situation than that. Medications can be a wonderful help in managing the symptoms of mental illness, but they are not a cure.

Living a healthy life when one is suffering from mental illness requires relying on the support or supervision of family or friends, good health habits like exercise and a solid sleep routine, and knowing the signs of a recurrence of symptoms or the possibility of a negative episode. Probably the best medicine for those with mental illness is the presence of a compassionate human being who they can rely on. The support of another person can make a marked difference for the better.

The term "mental illness" is used to describe persons with many different types of disorders, including schizophrenia, bipolar disorder, depression, intellectual disabilities (once called "mental retardation"), autism, or Down syndrome. The important thing to remember is that even though someone has a mental illness, we are all people who are made in God's image.

Recently, I learned firsthand how mental illness can affect someone. Last fall on a sunny afternoon, my friend Annie and I we were enjoying a pizza and a funny DVD when she started crying. I was shocked by this and asked what was wrong. Annie has bipolar disorder, and she knows her disease well. She explained that the change of seasons can trigger severe mood swings between periods of mania (energy) and periods of depression (like now.) Because she was proactive about her illness, this incident prompted her to call her doctor for an adjustment in her medications.

A person with mental illness can experience major changes in personality, difficulty functioning socially or coping with everyday problems, or have disturbing thoughts or feelings. One critical side effect of living with a mental illness is that its symptoms can cause people to be unemployed. The stress of full-time hours along with the everyday challenges of a job can be triggers that make it difficult for a person with mental illness to hold down a job.

God's Image

As Christians, we speak of respecting all life, but in reality, we often neglect people with mental illness. More than ever, our society is cutting back on funds for those with mental illness. About twenty years ago, there were mental health hospitals, children's services, and other health agencies that addressed the needs of people with mental illness. Today those places are rare. Resources for daily care are almost nonexistent. Although there are group homes and foster homes for people with mental disorders who cannot live on their own or with their families, these situations can be less than optimal alternatives for supporting a healthy life.

Addressing an international conference sponsored by the Pontifical Council for Pastoral Assistance to Health-Care Workers in November, 1996, Pope John Paul II said: "Whoever suffers from mental illness always bears God's image and likeness in themselves, as does every human being. In addition, they always have the inalienable right not only to be considered as an image of God and therefore a person, but also to be treated as such."[10]

Families with relatives who have mental illness can find their religious faith challenged. They live with uncertainty and anxiety as they can move from crisis to crisis. Here, the support of a faith community can be critical. In her work, Eve challenges parishes to make a concerted effort to include all those with disabilities along with their families, encouraging them to be a part of the parish and its ministries. On the other hand, ministers in the parish should see what needs exists that can be addressed for those with mental illness and their families.

St. Dymphna, who lived in the seventh century, is the Church's patron saint of people with mental illness or emotional disorders. May we remember all the Jennys and Jimmys and caregivers like Eve, and pray that we may be a source of comfort and support for them.

All persons with disabilities or special needs should be welcomed in the Church. Every person, however limited, is capable of growth in holiness.... Some persons with disabilities live in isolating conditions that make it difficult for them to participate in catechetical experiences. "Since provision of access to religious functions is a pastoral duty," parishes should make that much more effort to include those who may feel excluded....

The Church's pastoral response in such situations is to learn about the disability, offer support to the family, and welcome the child.[11]

—*The National Directory for Catechesis*

To Consider

- Do you think mental illness is different than other diseases? Are you uncomfortable being with someone who has a mental illness? Why or why not?
- Does your parish include ministries for those with mental illness? If it does not, is there anything you can do to remedy that situation?

Prayer

Creator God, maker of earth and my body, be with me as I walk the fragile journey of life with mental illness. I know others do not understand my disease, and sometimes neither do I or my family and friends. At times I feel so alone and misunderstood; help me be faithful to my treatment program even when I feel better. May I reach out for help when I feel darkness coming on. Help me, my God, have the stamina to live with my wellness plan. Give me the things I need as I face this darkness, which can burst out in light. Embrace me with your strength as I face my health problems. If I know you are with me, I can do it, I can thrive. I am not alone. Bless me, my God.

CHAPTER EIGHT

Helping Others Can Be Healing

After he had washed their feet, had put on his robe,
and had returned to the table, he said to them, "Do you
know what I have done to you? You call me Teacher
and Lord—and you are right, for that is what I am. So
if I, your Lord and Teacher, have washed your feet, you
also ought to wash one another's feet. For I have set
you an example, that you also should do as I have done
to you. Very truly, I tell you, servants are not greater
than their master, nor are messengers greater than the
one who sent them. If you know these things, you are
blessed if you do them."

—*John 13:12–17*

I was shocked and concerned: my friend, Mary Fran, had
just told me she was diagnosed with stage 1 non-Hodgkin's
lymphoma. I do not know why her diagnosis hit me so hard; I
work with people who have chronic disease and know sickness

is a part of life. Maybe it was that Mary Fran took care of her health by watching her diet and walking regularly for exercise. I think it was because it was someone I knew who was pretty healthy, yet she had still been diagnosed with a serious illness.

What shocked me even more was that right after her initial diagnosis, before she had decided on a course of therapy, she went back to work. Full-time! This time of initial diagnosis is often the time when people tell us to be "gentle with ourselves," to take as much time off as we need from work and to try not to worry about our involvement with anything. Depending on our diagnosis and the recommended therapy, we might need to take this course of action. But for some people, like Mary Fran, trying to remain focused on our life apart from illness can be just the thing for our spiritual and physical well-being.

Mary Fran, a Catholic Charities mental health therapist, said that work kept her "what lies ahead" thoughts under control. "Work was a blessing and a great distraction, a way to focus on other people's lives and not on how the disease would play out. It helped me to cope with the uncertainty of what would lie ahead." It helped her focus on others, and not entirely on herself. Work was a good part of her therapy plan because the day-to-day tasks and schedule helped to normalize her life.

After consultation with a hematologist and an oncologist, Mary Fran decided to undergo radiation, the preferred treatment in this case. She had thirteen consecutive radiation treatments on the lymph nodes in the neck area that were affected by the disease. She tolerated the treatment well, and was back at work one week after it ended.

We all have bodies that can be visited by health problems. We might live with the pain of arthritis, the challenge of diabetes or cancer, or the constant aches and pains of disintegrating joints. Our health is not our only concern, but it is front and center when we cannot perform the tasks of everyday life—like eating, dressing ourselves, or keeping our house clean.

But focusing only on our problems might not be the best thing for our health. St Paul echoes this thought when he writes, "Blessed be the God and Father of our Lord Jesus Christ, the Father of mercies and the God of all consolation, who consoles us in all our affliction, so that we may be able to console those who are in any affliction with the consolation with which we ourselves are consoled by God. For just as the sufferings of Christ are abundant for us, so also our consolation is abundant through Christ" (2 Corinthians 1:3–5).

Facing an illness brings its own challenges, such as getting to doctor's appointments, managing our medications, and doing physical therapy. Even our simple daily tasks seem to take more time: getting up in the morning, paying our bills, doing laundry, and cooking meals. Emotionally, we can be overwhelmed by all we need to do coupled with our anxiety about our future.

Yet, despite our sickness, we all can benefit from giving back, from volunteering, even if we have health problems.

Studies show that volunteers live longer, have higher func-
tional ability, lower rates of depression and less incidence of
heart disease, according to a study by the Corporation for
National and Community Service (www.nationalservice.gov).
Although sometimes people tell us to stay home, rest, and not
get involved, looking outside of our personal health care and
health setbacks can be a tremendous way to heal ourselves.

An occupational therapist friend of mine feels that when
patients volunteer, "It gives people who are ill a reason to get
up in the morning. Looking outward takes a person's awareness off constantly thinking about his or her condition. Patients
who see a purpose in their life usually fare better." People such
as this can experience less depression and fear.

Some of the "healthiest" patients, even among those who have
serious conditions, are those who move from self-absorption to
thinking of others. Even something small will do. Volunteering
for a non-profit organization by making phone calls or stuffing
envelopes can be a great way to start. It does not have to be a
huge task, but something that shifts our awareness and energy
to other people or other causes is a start.

Those who cannot get out of their homes can also do good
by acknowledging their caregivers or healthcare professionals.
Maybe it's thanking a family member or friend who always
calls or drops by for a cup of coffee. A simple phone call, a hug,
or just saying, "Thanks, I appreciate all you do for me," goes a
long way. A written note, a flower, or a cup of tea, or a candy

bar given to a caregiver can be a touching gift. Everyone needs to be affirmed and loved. Being healthy is a two-way street. The person receiving care needs to be of service, too.

According to Mark Drummond, a psychologist who specializes in personality disorders, "being 'self caring' is considered healthy, but many mistake that for being self-centered." Many health organizations are volunteer-driven. The National Multiple Sclerosis Society raises money for MS research, advocates for better client laws such as accessible housing, public buildings, and parking, and speeding up Social Security benefits. Funds have been raised and government policies have become laws all because of the efforts of persons with a passion for giving back.

Those living with cancer are invited to become involved in a program called "Anyone Who Believes." The organization challenges anyone touched by cancer to get involved with the motto, "The fight against cancer isn't up to somebody else. It's up 2 me. It's up 2 you. It's up 2 every single one of us." The energy of that movement is exciting and positive, and invites those with cancer to take control of living with their disease. Who better to do good or volunteer to help someone than a person who has the same disease, who is "in the club" and knows firsthand the feelings of discomfort, fear of the unknown, loneliness, or the side effects from medications than someone who has lived with or is living with disease?

The decision to go outward to others, away from focusing on our health alone, is one that we make ourselves. Others might invite us, but ultimately, we answer the question: What are we going to do? This is our test of faith: Will we be Good Samaritans to someone who needs our help? In the past, we might remember a time when we were not helped. Will we hold on to that hurtful memory and not help others? Many times in life, one mistake, one insensitive comment from another person finds us devastated. We might completely stop our activity or any social interaction with the person who offended us. Perhaps we bailed out of life when we became sick.

Each one of us has the power to decide what to do with the hurts and misunderstandings in our lives. Kevin Smith, an independent film director and comedian, was kicked off a Southwest Airlines airplane for being too fat. He admits to being humiliated at first, but then realized it was the best thing that ever happened to him. He said, "It felt like they stripped me of all my accomplishments by reducing me to a fat guy in a little chair on a plane." He figured he had two options: he could "Crumble, wither, die, and go away...or rise above it." He chose the latter.

Ever since he was ejected from the airline, Smith has taken back the power he lost that day and used it as fuel for an extraordinary career reinvention. He has produced television reality shows, comedy films, and written a self-help book. He has traveled across the United States by bus (not plane) to perform as a comedian at Radio City Music Hall and in Hollywood. He has gone to book signings in England—where he decided he had to "get over himself" and fly again. Whatever it is that makes a person take their negative life experience and do something positive about it, Kevin Smith has it.

Comforting Prayers

We need to respond to the tough stuff in life with our hearts and minds, of course, but also with our souls. Can we take our negative and difficult health problems and respond in a creative, healthy way? Can we turn around something physically challenging and create something good for others and ultimately, ourselves? That takes faith.

"When I fretted," Mary Fran reflected, "the following Scripture passage was the spiritual equivalent of a deep breath: 'Cast your burden on the LORD, and he will sustain you; he will never permit the righteous to be moved'" (Psalm 55:22). To set her priorities straight regarding the place of good health in the scheme of life, she prayed: "Because your steadfast love is better than life, my lips will praise you" (Psalm 63:3). Along with her Scripture prayers, Mary Fran said a daily rosary and put herself under the protection of Our Lady of Lourdes, asking that she be put (figuratively) into the healing waters of Lourdes.

Connecting with others brings hope into our lives. Mary Fran noted a real sense of solidarity that grew with those she encountered in the waiting area of the radiation oncology department.

No pain pill, bandage, or surgery can help another along the road to good health and recovery like the gift of presence, of simply being there. She moved from self-absorption about herself to a little more balanced awareness of her brothers and sisters.

Sometimes our health limitations keep us from volunteering or ministering to others. But we need to keep focused on the idea of giving back, and looking outside of our health situations can be a part of this. Maybe the giving back will happen in a matter of months or in a year. Deciding what to do, when to do it, and even if we should get involved might be an exciting but challenging decision for us. We have to make that decision within spiritual discernment. We can follow our hearts, talk with friends and family, and spend time with our God, asking for guidance in this important part of our recovery.

Mary Fran reflects on the powerful social rewards of being involved outside of our own little world: "One day I was waiting for treatment in the Mayo Clinic's reception area for the radiation oncology unit when a man came walking through and, with vigor, gonged the bell signaling that he completed treatment. In unison, the room cheered."

A high school senior summed it up well when she was the featured volunteer on a local TV news "Making a Difference" spot. She said she was inspired by the words of poet Emily Dickinson, who wrote, "If I can stop one heart from breaking, I shall not live in vain." This is good spiritual advice for everyone.

I always wondered why somebody doesn't do something about that. Then I realized I was somebody.[12]

—*Lily Tomlin*

To Consider

- Are you drawn to helping others in some way? What is it that you would most like to do?
- Do your friends and family support your decision to volunteer? If not, who might you call on to help you with your efforts?

Prayer

Creator God, maker of earth and our bodies, I am ready to continue my path to healing. I am restless and want to reach out to others, as they so kindly did to me. I ask you to help that I may bring life and hope to my brothers and sisters who are in need of companionship. I offer most of all, my simple presence with them, to simply be with them, as they face a time of uncertainty. I do not have all the answers, but I am willing to be there for them. I know you are with us and we trust we will be all right. Together we ask you to bless us, O steadfast God.

CHAPTER NINE

Pumping Up With Prayer and Exercise

Or do you not know that your body is a temple of the Holy Spirit within you, which you have from God, and that you are not your own? For you were bought with a price; therefore glorify God in your body.
—*1 Corinthians 6:19–20*

We pray in Church, before our meals, at anniversaries, and before surgeries. Some people pray before they play bingo. We bless our pets on the feast of St. Francis, acknowledging that our God is deeply imbedded in all the things in our world. God is intimately woven into our physical and spiritual lives. That is why our health issues must be integrated and woven together with our spiritual lives. We need to bring our faith into the marketplace of our daily lives.

We pretty much know what to do to take care of our medical needs. We watch our sodium or carbohydrates, and take our prescriptions according to the directions on our pharmacy bottles. We see our doctors for our annual physical appointments, and follow through on any blood work or tests, scans, or x-rays that our doctor recommends. Even though a doctor might be a great medical technician or diagnostician, he or she probably does not prescribe prayer and exercise as an integral part of our overall wellness plan.

We know that exercise is good for our hearts, minds, and bodies. Activity can be healing on many levels. So what about praying when we exercise? Many people find that praying during exercise is the perfect place to contemplate, meditate, and clear their minds—and to stay healthy. Indeed, Scripture talks about both spiritual and physical exercise. In 1 Timothy 4:7b–8 we hear, "Train yourself in godliness, for, while physical training is of some value, godliness is valuable in every way, holding promise for both the present life and the life to come."

According to the Mayo Clinic staff, regular physical activity has many benefits and can improve our lives. Everyone can do some sort of exercise. We can exercise or engage in some form of physical activity regardless of our age or physical ability. Think of people you know who went through a serious illness, surgery, or cancer regimes. They might still cook at home, drive to church, or attend meetings or movies outside of their homes. Conventional wisdom might tell us they needed to stay home and rest, but other schools of thought say that by keeping active, they are doing something to help them recover faster. Most types of physical activity have great health benefits. Our exercise does not have to be a complex program that we do at a gym outside of our homes. Some simple things like walking in place inside our homes, stretching when we get up in the morning, or following an exercise program on TV is a great start. Just to be sure you can safely handle the activity; it is a good idea to talk to your healthcare professional to let them know what you plan to do. As a matter of safety, check in with your doctor to make sure that an activity is appropriate for your specific health conditions.

Exercise is a profound commitment to our bodies. Steve Yzerman, former Detroit Red Wings hockey forward, says, "I'm exhausted trying to stay healthy." By exercising, we can control and maintain our weight, or lose weight if we need to. Exercise can combat health conditions such as heart disease or high blood pressure. Being active boosts high-density lipoprotein (HDL), the "good" cholesterol, and decreases unhealthy triglycerides. It enables your blood to flow smoothly, which decreases the risk of cardiovascular disease. Physical activity can help prevent or manage many health concerns: stroke, type 2 diabetes, and certain types of cancer, as well as ease arthritis.

Activity can improve our moods and emotions by stimulating various brain chemicals that can leave us more relaxed and happier. Regular physical exercise can improve muscle strength and stamina. Our cardiovascular systems can work more efficiently when we exercise. Many people have difficulty falling and staying asleep. Regular exercise can help you fall asleep faster and sleep deeper. Exercise can be fun, an activity that helps us unwind and connects us with others.

Integrating Prayer With Exercise

When we exercise or work out for our physical health, our spirituality can easily be woven into any routine, no matter how simple or complex. The whole idea of doing physical activity for our overall wellbeing can be a simple addition to our prayer lives. It need not be expensive: we do not have to join a fancy gym or buy lots of workout equipment to be fit. It can start by doing simple things each day.

Psychologist, author, and bodybuilder Kevin Vost explains that God's command to "Be perfect" applies not only to our moral lives, but our physical lives, too. He has authored several Christian fitness books where he explains that the stronger and more beautiful we make our bodies, which are temples of the Holy Spirit (see 1 Corinthians 6:19), "the better we imitate Christ—in whom perfect strength, endurance and beauty were incarnated."[13]

Although exercising makes us feel good, stronger, helps our backs and knees feel a little better, is a discipline. It might be the last thing we want to do on a dreary day, or when we feel achy or tired. Prayer can help us get over these humps. As noted on an exercise website, "Simple Christian prayers invite believers to seek God as they begin a workout routine, heal from a strenuous exercise, and struggle to keep exercising for good health."[14]

Prayer and exercise fit together well. When we move our bodies we can mirror the actions with various prayers and sacred words. Exercise brings a repetition and rhythm that complements prayer perfectly. As she exercises, my friend, Sr. Sharon, breathes in and out using the "Jesus Prayer". She inhales deeply and says, "Lord Jesus Christ, Son of the living God," and as she exhales she says, "Have mercy on me a sinner." She uses this prayer when she walks, and notes that it can be shortened to a simple "Jesus, mercy."

Many people work out on treadmills or use weight machines, and pray a simple sentence such as, "Bless me, God, and all my friends." The rhythm of the exercise you are doing can determine what kind of prayer fits or works into your routine. Yoga offers a fluid process that lends itself to reflective prayers and music. I pray the Taize verse, "Jesus, remember me, when you come into your kingdom" as I do my daily morning stretches.

Some people work out after they have finished their workday. They put an exercise DVD or workout tape on their television or computer, and give themselves over to the movement. Some people turn off the sound and play religious hymns or reflections as they exercise along to the tape. Others simply pray a mantra or favorite prayer repeatedly as they move.

You can also use an iPod or MP3 player for inspiration as you exercise. There are several creative resources available from exercise experts who have woven prayer into their physical routines. Prayer and exercise songs, programs, and books are available online, at fitness centers, or in religious bookstores.

For those who like to start their exercise with prayer, there is a resource called Pray-as-You-Go, a free daily meditation from Jesuit Media Initiatives. It offers, short, ten-to-twelve minute meditations on the daily readings with bells or music in the background, and can be downloaded to an MP3 player, tablet, or computer. Some people put on their Pray-as-You-Go podcasts and walk in place at home before their evening meals. The podcasts bring together music, a passage of scripture and a few questions for personal reflection in their daily sessions. The music and prayers can have a calming effect on those working out.

A podcast might offer a short breathing exercise and an optional physical exercise segment. The guided breathing exercise can lower blood pressure and relax the body after a tense day at work. Breathing exercises can help people sleep better. These can all be adapted to your own personal needs, schedule, and interests. These podcasts can help you slow down and review after a hectic, active day.

My friend Pat has an iPad filled with classic Christian songs like *How Great Thou Art* and *Be Not Afraid*. She listens to that music as she goes about her daily tasks such as cleaning, folding the laundry, walking the dog, and traveling to the doctor. She says she likes to do twenty minutes of stretching accompanied by these songs before she starts her day. She and her grandson, a high school football player, e-mail each other about new apps that they find for Christian workouts.

The Rosary Workout is another program that combines physical exercise with prayer. It is a well-structured, methodical, easy-to-follow, and result-producing program that incorporates cardiovascular training with prayerful meditation through the rosary.

We have been called to exercise for years. It is nothing new to us. Many of us remember the physical fitness trend that started in the 1960s with President John F. Kennedy, who said, "Physical fitness is not only one of the most important keys to a healthy body, it is the basis of dynamic and creative intellectual activity."[15] Earlier, Pope Pius XII reflected, "The highest merit should not be attributed to him who has the strongest and most agile muscles, but rather to him who shows the most steady ability in keeping them subject to the power of the spirit."[16]

We are challenged to keep our bodies, these temples of the Holy Spirit, in good working order. Exercise can bring a host of physical and psychological benefits. When we add a layer of prayer, we can benefit spiritually, too. Exercising is just as important as taking our pills and seeing our physicians. It is a healthy call to be faithful stewards of our total health. Praying during our workouts can be a powerful blend of motor and faith skills. It is a creative, blessed gift to our whole person.

I chuckle at French philosopher Montaigne's comment, "To strengthen the mind, you must harden the muscles."[17] This is not far away from the Scripture directive to "pray always."

There is a need to find free time in order to exercise strength and dexterity, endurance, and harmonious movement, so as to attain or guarantee that physical efficiency necessary to man's overall equilibrium.[18]

—*Pope John Paul II*

To Consider

- Do you try to exercise regularly? If not, what keeps you from exercise?
- Is there a friend or neighbor that you can exercise with, maybe even taking a walk together for twenty minutes or so a day?

Prayer

Creator God, maker of earth and my body, give me the discipline to keep my body limber and healthy with exercise. Let me remember how happy and good I feel after I exercise and pray to you. Let that memory keep me coming back to my exercise routine on days when I want to skip it for a nap, a snack, or watching television. Let me take care of my body by coming back to exercise so I can nurture it to the glory of your name. I will try to be a good steward of my body with your help. I am not alone. Bless me, my God.

CHAPTER TEN

When Your Suffering Can't Be Seen

Do not judge, so that you may not be judged. For with the judgment you make you will be judged, and the measure you give will be the measure you get. Why do you see the speck in your neighbor's eye, but do not notice the log in your own eye?

—*Matthew 7:1–3*

I was at a high school class reunion and so many of my classmates looked great! Most were tan, well dressed, and happy. Everyone seemed to be wearing new clothes; their hair was styled and looked good. After the initial joyful greetings and family updates, I talked to a few of them one-on-one, and people told me their personal stories. Many were suffering from some serious health problems, and it made me remember that appearances can be deceiving.

The mobility problems were easy to spot: Some of my former classmates used canes, wheelchairs, or walkers. Others had an uneven gait when they walked, or they limped; they were the ones living with knee replacements or arthritis. Many wore glasses, and one person used an oxygen tank to breathe. Some of my classmates who looked fine on the outside were suffering from invisible health problems. They were frustrated when people said things like, "You are lucky that you are in great health!"

When we do not see someone's symptoms, we might assume that they are not suffering. Just because we cannot see a symptom does not mean that one does not exist, or as an online chat group participant Carolyn Dross, says, "My family seems to assume that if they can't see it, there really is nothing wrong with me." Yet non-obvious symptoms are very real, and are often referred to as invisible, hidden, or silent symptoms.

When we see someone with a cast on their arm, using a walker, or sitting in a wheelchair, we know immediately that something is going on with their health. We visually get the message that a person has a health issue.

Health industry advertisers spend lots of money using pictures and stories to promote their products. A commercial that sells a product that promises relief from joint pain or a drug that slows the progression of a chronic disease might show photos of people dancing, jogging, or gardening—anything that makes them look disease-free. As a marketing tool, using people with obvious medical conditions tells too much of their story. Advertisers need to use upbeat images that show activity, happiness, and health. They want to hide a symptom, implying that if you cannot see the pain, it does not exist.

Just because we see someone with an obvious sign of a health problem does not mean we know or understand that person's limitations. People who live with mobility challenges can often function quite well and work very well in the outside world. It is a fact that many other hidden health problems can cause people to lose their jobs more than using a wheelchair—cognitive problems, mental illness symptoms, and other chronic conditions can cause people to lose their jobs. Some invisible health problems can seriously challenge people to do the simple tasks of everyday life.

There is a dichotomy between how you look and how you may feel. Some hidden health problems can include fatigue, fibromyalgia, mental illness, visual problems, confusion and forgetfulness, stiffness, bladder problems, chronic pain—the list goes on. With these health problems, we do not immediately perceive that a person is suffering medically.

I use an electric cart because of my mobility problems caused by my multiple sclerosis. I drive an adapted van, still work, shop, and cook. A friend who was recently diagnosed with MS shared with me that she was limiting her driving since she experienced severe vertigo (dizziness, light headedness) more and more frequently. She asked me if I still drove since I was more disabled than she. I told her that the vertigo was not one of my MS symptoms. My walking limitations were, and they were obvious. But I could drive with my hand controls. Just because we cannot see someone's symptoms—like her dizziness—does not mean they are not real, and affect their everyday lives. On the other hand, just because we see a symptom does not tell us what a person's limitations might be.

One of the greatest challenges about hidden symptoms is that unless you choose to tell people what is bothering you, they do not know that anything is wrong. That might be fine, but if you are asked to do an extra project at work, volunteer, or attend evening functions, you might decline because of your health. People may then judge you and think you are not doing your part or are lazy. As such, it is often better to be honest about our limitations than to invite unfair criticism or judgment. When you "disclose" your illness, you are not complaining or eliciting pity. It is human weakness to judge others, and sometimes others do judge us and think we are being lazy or not a "team player." Only we can decide how to handle our own situations.

There are hundreds of invisible symptoms that people live with and others might not know about. Some people might struggle at their jobs with hearing loss, chronic back pain, cancer, incontinence, emotional illness, or neuralgia. At different stages of the illness, a person might look perfectly healthy to others. Telling someone about our health problem can first of all, share our burden. Bottling up something that we live with all the time can ease a little of the anxiety we might have while coping with our health.

A friend of mine tries to divert the tension of whether to tell others about our health challenges with a funny quote, "Most people are quite happy to suffer in silence, if they are sure everybody knows they are doing it." There is a lot of truth to that statement!

Others might be willing to quietly help us out in a discreet way—if our knees are acting up, they might just get our mail and leave it at our desk. If we are not feeling well because of nausea due to medications, a friend might bring some water or crackers to us. Telling others can also help them realize that we are limited in what we can do. If we are struggling with chronic back pain and tell our church social committee, they will understand why we do not sign up for the committee that decorates the church with wreaths and garland at Christmas. We cannot climb a ladder. It might be a courtesy to tell others why we are not seemingly doing "our part."

On the other hand, we have to be very honest and sensitive to other people's feelings, too. Everyone has something that might keep them from doing their part at work or socially. We must be honest not to use our health in a way that takes advantage of those who are healthier than we are. It is a delicate balance to have someone take over our duties when we might be well enough some days to go bowling! We need to look at how other people feel and perceive us. How would we feel if the tables were switched and our friend was asking us to do more and more for them when we were not feeling well that day?

How would we feel if they were taking part in what we felt was socially "fun" stuff and said they could not do their jobs?

Having an invisible health problem not only causes a person pain and challenges in their everyday tasks of living, but it also adds a challenge to what we actually can do in the world—physically, emotionally and socially. It seems like honesty on the part of both the person with the invisible symptoms and the persons in their lives needs to work so that each can kindly tell the other how they feel, what they perceive is going on, and how they can be of service to each other. Both parties need to honestly share their views.

So, it might be good to tell a few coworkers or neighbors about our health. We could share our own bottled-up emotions and frustrations about looking good but feeling less than healthy. We also need personal "health integrity" and honestly do what we can. Using health for an excuse for not doing our part is dishonest and can bring about the habit of using our diseases dishonestly. People are perceptive—they know when a person has a real need and when they do not.

Judge Not

I overheard two people talking a few weeks ago. One woman said she was experiencing fatigue. Her companion responded in a fifteen-minute talk, "I get tired, too!" There is a big difference between being tired at the end of the day and experiencing the overwhelming fatigue following chemotherapy or chronic fatigue syndrome.

Others might judge us—and we might judge others—because no one knows what is going on inside our bodies. It is a daily challenge for all with hidden symptoms to balance how we feel inside and how we look outside. Sometimes, we might wonder if we are imagining these aches and pains ourselves.

If others tell every detail of their medical history, I try to remember that our medical and physical story is only one part of our life. We are spiritual, emotional, social beings. We are not taking into account the other parts of our bodies. I also believe that I need to stop talking about my health problems. I catch myself talking about my MS, and then I try to be quiet. It is a habit I am consciously trying to limit. This is really treating your neighbor as you would want to be treated!

I am getting better at thinking about my neighbor. When I see someone who looks perfectly healthy to me (usually a person who parks a sport utility vehicle in a handicapped space and jumps out to enter a store) I immediately judge him or her. I get angry and wonder why they parked in a space I or another person who has limited mobility would need! It really is a matter of trust on my part. I do not know if the person has heart disease, asthma, or another problem. It is not about me.

The possibility that a person might have a number of invisible symptoms puts me in my judgmental place, but I challenge myself, too. I make certain that I do all I can do to help my brothers and sisters at work or as a volunteer. I vow to never judge another person...although I slip. Sometimes I go to a person who looks healthy and I tell them outright that I judge them. I tell them I think they are not doing their part and are using their disease as an excuse.

And then I apologize for my lack of trust and ask them to forgive me.

I pray for them and their health needs, and I ask God to forgive me and bless me. I ask God that I remember that even though a person does not look sick, they might be struggling with an invisible chronic medical problem and struggling to live well. I feel at peace with a God who is so understanding and forgiving...and healing.

Elvis Presley sang the classic song, "Walk a Mile in My Shoes." One line from it says a lot: "Before you abuse, criticize and accuse—walk a mile in my shoes."[19]

> Do not judge your neighbor until you walk two moons in his moccasins.[19]
>
> —*Cheyenne Indian folklore*

To Consider

- Do you have medical conditions that cannot be seen? Would you like others to know about them? Why?
- How do you respond if others say, "you look good" when you really feel sick?

Prayer

Creator God, maker of earth and my body, bless me with health of mind and body as I face the day-to-day challenge of wavering health. I am embarrassed to admit I do not hear or see or walk as well as I used to. I do not want others to know that my back hurts, my hands cannot open packages easily any more, and I get so nervous when I drive. You know when I am sick whether I look sick or not—and you are with me. Let me accept my hidden health challenges, and let me support others in their weakness, too. Teach me not to judge others. Bless me with facing my health with integrity and hope. If I know you are with me, I can go ahead. I am not alone. Bless me, my God.

CHAPTER ELEVEN

Making Sense of Suffering

And not only that, but we also boast in our sufferings,
knowing that suffering produces endurance, and
endurance produces character, and character produces
hope, and hope does not disappoint us, because God's
love has been poured into our hearts through the Holy
Spirit that has been given to us.

—*Romans 5:3–5*

I was alone, helpless, and vulnerable—then I panicked and
screamed for God.

My doctor's had office had called and left a message on my
home answering machine on a Friday afternoon. I had to retake
a medical test. I got the message when I got home from work
after business hours. The earliest I could call to reschedule was
Monday morning. I was angry at the insensitivity of the nurse
who called and left a message at that time—I wondered who
trains these people!

It was the first time I had to retake a medical test; that in-between time of waiting and insecurity was harder to endure than my certain diagnosis of MS over three decades ago. After my test and the whole ordeal were over, I learned from others that retaking medical tests was often due to technical errors and happened somewhat regularly. But I did not know that at the time and was frantic.

That weekend seemed to last for months. I replayed the message at least ten times. I was afraid of cancer and imagined only the worst. I was so nervous all weekend I could not eat or sleep. A few friends told me that it would be fine, that it was just a routine procedure, to retake medical tests. I remembered the old saying, "every medical test or surgery is routine—unless it is yours!" Family and friends tried to support and comfort me but it only masked my anxiety. It was still my medical test coming up.

I scheduled the test for Tuesday morning. Tuesday could not come soon enough for me.

So much of our suffering is emotional; it is in our hearts and heads. The anxiety we take with us before a medical test, outpatient procedure, or treatment plan—can bring us over-whelming and non-stop anxiety. We are extremely vulnerable at these times, and although family and friends might try to ease our obsessing about the situation, we take it with us. We do not experience this kind of nervousness that often. How many times do we face a medical procedure, serious diagnostic tests, or a conference with our physician about a medical prognosis? These are life-changing events and it is only human to be concerned.

Friends offered to drive me to my test, but I wanted to go alone. I remember feeling that this was my "stuff." Sometimes I like having a companion for a medical test, but for this one I remember I wanted to be alone with God. While I waited for the radiologist to interpret the results, I felt completely empty. I either had cancer or not. I could not do anything about it. I was powerless.

Then, my panic gave way to a rush of peace. I think the Spirit moved me from fear of the unknown to the certainty of God in my life. I did not give up, but I let go. A spiritual calmness came, and I knew that I was deeply with God in that medical office, sitting next to the cold metal machines.

If I had cancer, it would show up on the test. It was out of my hands. I was peaceful, feeling that I took this possible life-changing event and entered into the heart of God because of it. I experienced an intense, almost passionate love of God at that time. I remember feeling an intimate union with God. I felt what it meant to call on God, to hope in God, to just want to be in God's arms. I felt safe.

Some persons say that their illness is a gift from God, and others say it is not. I tend to not argue about whether having a chronic disease is a gift from God—I just know that having to face the outcome of that medical test drew me to deeply reach out to God. This was not at the depth level of my daily prayer—it was much deeper, an intimate communion. I literally and passionately fell into God. I am not a theologian—I do not try to explain why God allows suffering in our world. I know God as the Creator. Nature is not perfect, and sometimes our bodies are not perfect either. I try to take my body, my health where it is and go on from there.

The Spirituality of Coping

Everyone deals with suffering differently, but for many of us, spirituality can blend with our suffering quite well. I know I depend on my faith especially in matters of my health. As people of faith, suffering can lead us to the Gospel because we need our God desperately. Suffering lets us act on our need to depend on God. When we deal with serious life situations, we can choose to honestly face ourselves and be transformed by the power and strength of God's love.

Julian of Norwich, a fourteenth-century mystic who had very little formal education but had profound life wisdom reflects on a way to view suffering. She reflects that God did not say, "You will not be troubled," or, "You will not be tempted," or, "You will not be distressed." He said, "You will not be overcome." I am touched by that—we have power over everything in our lives! We can take our suffering, not change it, but control what we do with it.

Suffering can call each of us to become stronger persons emotionally and spiritually. It can also deepen us because we literally stand before God honestly and with pure need. This vulnerability that suffering brings can speak of true hope in our God. Everything is stripped away from us, we are not in control, and whatever God gives is gift to us.

The words of Psalm 27: 8–9 soothed me before my test: "'Come,' my heart says, 'seek his face!' Your face, LORD, do I seek. Do not hide your face from me. Do not turn your servant away in anger, you who have been my help. Do not cast me off, do not forsake me, O God of my salvation!" I prayed this psalm repeatedly and it comforted me so I relaxed a bit.

I think the biggest help for me when I face a medical test result or the worsening of my symptoms is prayer. Prayer changes my attitude about health problems—my own prayer and the many people who pray for me. Before I have a medical test, a doctor's appointment, or take my injections, I remember anyone touched by this disease called MS or any living with cancer or any disease. I pray for all who suffer from any illness, mental or physical. Prayer, for me, is probably the safest, oldest non-invasive healing proactive response to medical suffering in my life.

In my bedroom I have a prayer space. I light a candle, and take time to meditate. I pray the psalms and am always struck by the ones that speak of healing. The psalms comfort me and help me put sickness and suffering into perspective. I thank God that I can still do all I do after decades of living with MS and that I have loving friends, a wonderful sister, and a sense of humor. Prayer shifts my thinking from what I can't do to what I can. Of course, I realize that even with all the new medications out, there still isn't a cure, but I can still pray. And so I do. Here are some of the things I pray for that day:

I pray for all those who have cancer or congestive heart failure or mental illness or Parkinson's disease. I think of the many whose sufferings challenge their quality of life, and how they struggle to get out of bed each morning to go to work, or sometimes just to get dressed each day. I pray for friends whom I know who will be diagnosed with serious illness in the future.

I pray for their family and caregivers. I ask special blessings on all caregivers. Whether it is a child who brings a portable phone or glass of milk to a parent, or a spouse who helps with cooking and laundry chores, I remember them and hold them especially in my heart.

For years people with diseases have used prayer, music, ritual imagination and faith along with traditional therapies to cope with their disease. Over many years, I have learned that prayer lets me transform suffering. I am changed, converted by prayer. My suffering or the suffering of my family or friends does not go away—but it is different. I am different and changed by my response to the suffering.

Sometimes, doctors, nurses and other medical specialists are portrayed by society and the media as being skeptical of prayer in management of disease. But in my experience, my medical professionals support me in my beliefs. I rest, do physical therapy, take my medicine, and pray. I am faithful to praying through my suffering. I do not know the grand theology of what I am asking my God, but I faithfully ask my creator for a daily cure and presence in my suffering. When I feel I am with God and not alone, I can bear challenging medical tests, procedures, and an uncertain health future.

God Is in the Suffering

The poor, the hungry, the grieving, and those who suffer are blessed because their lack of self-sufficiency is obvious to them every day. They must turn somewhere for strength. People who are rich, successful, and beautiful may go through life relying on their natural gifts. But people who are needy, dependent, and dissatisfied with life are more likely to welcome God's free gift of love. At times when we hit "rock bottom" our suffering can change us as we realize God's closeness to us in our pain, that Jesus had chosen to suffer for love of us.

When we celebrate birthdays, anniversaries, graduations, we pray to our God in thanksgiving, sometimes asking for a blessing on the new phase of our lives. These moments are joyous—we are on the mountain with God and want to stay there because everything is so good. But the reality is we cannot stay up there where everything is good. Jesus leads us down the mountain as he led Peter and the disciples: "As they were coming down the mountain, he ordered them to tell no one about what they had seen, until after the Son of Man had risen from the dead. So they kept the matter to themselves, questioning what this rising from the dead could mean" (Mark 9:9–10)

Down from the mountain, we enter the real world. We celebrated the good and happy times on top of the mountain, and we must also deal with the reality when we come down. There might be a lot of trials, challenges and suffering before we experience the delight and peace from the mountaintop. Peter and Jesus were transformed after they experienced suffering and death. This is the progression for every Christian: faith, suffering, and glory.

When we are diagnosed with an illness or have been involved in a car accident, we need to bring God into our midst even more so. Suffering is part of our human story. Christ was human, and he showed us, really, that we can endure suffering. It is not easy or pleasant, but we cannot have the glory without coming down from the mountain and entering our real world, a world where people are sick, lonely, confused, and poor. The way to peace and glory is through the frustrations, sadness, failures, and pain of following Christ in our everyday life. Peter and the disciples saw this progression from suffering to glory in Jesus's death and resurrection, and in their lives. It is the progression in our lives, too.

My test showed that I did not have cancer. But since this experience, I reach out to anyone who does, and keep them tucked in my heart and prayer. Sometimes I tell them how fearful I was, and how I thrust my fear and entered more deeply into my God.

The theme of death in Christianity is not about dying or suffering for its own sake. It is about being born to love, to be outgoing to be self-giving. When I let my self-interest and self-centeredness die, I choose a full life.

My suffering drove me to my God. I let God in and the result was peace—and glory.

> For me, almost the best litmus test of whether a person has healthy or unhealthy religion is, "What do they do with their pain?"[21]
>
> —*Richard Rohr*

To Consider

- What was your first reaction to your diagnosis? Did you ask God why sickness happens, and to you?
- What do you hope to do with your pain? Does your suffering make sense to your life?

Prayer

Creator God, maker of earth and my body, let me face this suffering honestly and with deep faith. I know it will take time for me to deal with this shock and vulnerability in my life. Bless me with patience and calm my ever-anxious heart. Let me accept my feelings—my tears and silence, my outbursts and anger. I feel powerless as I face and grieve over more and more losses in my life. Help me, my God, have the courage to be able to come down the mountain and transform my suffering into glory. Help me to do something creative with my pain. If

I know you are with me, I can go ahead. I am not alone. Bless me, my God.

CHAPTER TWELVE

Embracing Our Losses

In this you rejoice, even if now for a little while you have had to suffer various trials, so that the genuineness of your faith—being more precious than gold that, though perishable, is tested by fire—may be found to result in praise and glory and honor when Jesus Christ is revealed. Although you have not seen him, you love him; and even though you do not see him now, you believe in him and rejoice with an indescribable and glorious joy, for you are receiving the outcome of your faith, the salvation of your souls.

—1 Peter 1:6–9

Loretta was in her eighties and lived for over forty years in her Detroit home. Her four grown children lived in four different states, and her husband of over fifty years had died two years before. Loretta grew up as the only girl in a family of five brothers. She saw them pass away over the years, too.

Loretta had slowed down, did not have the physical stamina of her middle years, had undergone two cataract surgeries, a heart catheterization, and due to the loss of balance that often comes with aging, walked a little slower. Always an avid shopper, she no longer wanted to traverse the malls and department stores with her daughters looking for bargains.

Despite her slowing down, Loretta still served on parish committees, shared her strong religious and moral values with her children and grandchildren, cooked and baked their favorite meals when they visited, gave gifts of money rather than merchandise, and kept in regular touch by telephone. Her legacy of generosity grew strong, even during this time of physical diminishment and life on a fixed income. Loretta may have undergone many losses since her youth, but she still shared wisdom, presence, and her own talents with friends and family. During her time of life changes she was faithful to her spirituality: she loved the rosary and her parish Mass, and prayed from her own prayer book each day.

Losses in our lives are inevitable. Sometimes we face professional losses—we are fired, demoted, quit, search for more meaningful work, and never realize our professional dreams. We lose our status and drift away from our work colleagues. Other losses might be personal: A marriage may end in divorce; a lifelong friend may relocate across the country; our children move far away. We experience health losses too. Our bodies are constantly changing, and we lose basic functions we used to take for granted—hearing, eyesight, strength, coordina-tion, and even memory. In the eyes of society, those with some losses—the elderly, those who cannot work due to disabili-ties, those who have lost their jobs and status—are considered useless or powerless.

One of my sisters, Mary Lou, has struggled with the devas-tating effects of multiple sclerosis for many years. She lives in a nursing home and is dependent on people for bathing, eating dressing—all the activities of her daily life. Her spirit and outlook are upbeat. I asked her which of her losses affected her most over the years. She mentioned, "My right leg was pretty weak. I had trouble in the classroom teaching because of it. Then, I had to give up driving for safety reasons. They all came one after another...." Her losses kept coming. Physical changes gave way to stopping work and social activities over a period of time. Despite her utter dependence on others for her daily life, Mary Lou's spirituality keeps her happy. She is a role model for me and many others because she has changed her losses into a deep new spiritual life.

Sometimes we lose our family: a parent, spouse, or a child—to death or alienation; other times we lose an old, dear friend. In spite of—and along with our losses— we are invited to strive for holiness and health amid the broken circumstances of our lives. In today's challenging economic times, people lose jobs that they have had for a number of years. They struggle with not only the loss of income, but with the status or integrity it brought, the loss of health insurance and retirement benefits, the loss of social connections and professional friends, and the possible future losses of their homes, cars, or lifestyle.

All these changes in our lives can deeply shake our faith. They can become "spiritual emergencies." However, we are invited to find holiness and health amid the broken circumstances of our lives. Losses introduce vulnerability into our lives. It seems that we respond to our faith more intensely during our "loss" times. We are vulnerable at times of illness or during other personal problems. Getting right into the loss, facing it and embracing it and meeting our God right in the powerlessness of the loss helps us change into a transformed person. We go through the experience and come out seeing things in a new way. After a bout with heart surgery or surviving a serious accident, we see our lives in a different perspective.

Our loss can completely change us since we meet our God in our most vulnerable way and ask for strength. Jesus transforms us, and we are changed by his power. Going through our loss can be us going through our own Passover and Paschal Mystery. It is Christ who shows us that he is there to strengthen us and offer us hope and he will sustain us. This whole abandoning ourselves into God is freeing and puts our spiritual lives into perspective.

Many times the loss we have to face is part of our everyday life. We might delay a medical change to avoid a loss. After a surgery, we might lose some strength. Moving to assisted living means losing our homes and years of memories. Giving up a driver's license means a loss of independence. Taking a medical leave might mean losing our job and identity.

We have no control over some losses. We can only be honest about it, acknowledge it and move on, embracing the messiness and uncertainty. The words from Matthew 6:25–26 touch on this: "Therefore I tell you, do not worry about your life, what you will eat or what you will drink, or about your body, what you will wear. Is not life more than food, and the body more than clothing? Look at the birds of the air; they neither sow nor reap nor gather into barns, and yet your heavenly Father feeds them. Are you not of more value than they?"

After a feared medical procedure is over, people express a common reaction: "If I only knew then what I know now, I would have done it years ago." When we lose something we are stripped and seemingly weak and vulnerable. It might be the first time we face a profound personal tragedy; we are stripped of our health or independence—or something. That is the time of paradox—when we are open before our God and can say "now what?" That is just the time God is with us and transforms our suffering into a new us. We have been changed by this challenge and we are new in our God if we are open to God and ask for healing, for transformation. We resonate with the scriptural theme of when I am weak, I am strong.

If we do not try to change with God in the middle of our losses, we might try to deal with them in other ways. We might deny or ignore what is happening in our life, not talking about it, not bringing it to God. We might think that not facing it will make it go away. Perhaps we try to take matters into our own hands, and try to "fix" our loss by resorting to self medications and medical practices, or engaging in social behavior that we think might take care of other losses. Some of us may make our loss an obsession. We might only live, speak, read, or buy things that are directly related to our loss. These ways of coping seem to bring a quick fix, but fundamentally, in our core, in our hearts, we need to face our losses honestly, and go to our God.

When we are honest with what is happening in our lives, and we can see an event is challenging us, we become vulnerable. The sickness, family crisis, or problem can cause us to become vulnerable and we can allow this event to influence us. We then can choose how to deal with our vulnerability, but going to our God is a way to embrace the loss. In the middle of our sufferings and confusion, in the darkness and messiness of our life, Jesus gifts us with a new life: "and it is no longer I who live, but it is Christ who lives in me. And the life I now live in the flesh I live by faith in the Son of God, who loved me and gave himself for me" (Galatians 2:20).

Spiritual Emergencies

All of our transitions, losses, or changes can become moments that will challenge us to reflect on our human journey and simultaneously, provide us with the grounds for spiritual change.

The losses we experience have three distinct characteristics: (1) an ending; (2) a period of distress and confusion leading to (3) a new beginning. What is important is the journey through these three stages. How do we emerge from suffering in our lives and move to wisdom and love? Our challenges are not evils but blessings—the pivotal points which allow us to transform our lives with wisdom and acceptance.

In our life journey, we can feel abandoned and broken. Jesus on his journey was rejected, abandoned, betrayed, and crucified. Through the mystery of Jesus and the cross Jesus has risen to new life. Through our life losses, we are given new life. For those of us who have been excluded, considered worthless and overlooked, there is no place to go but "up." It can be very freeing not to have to play the life games of power, possessions, and prestige. We come to our God with our hearts and lives. We are transformed and see what matters in life in a new way.

Francis of Assisi, like Jesus his model, completely embraced his humanity. Francis suffered and experienced human betrayal. Despite Francis's pain, he fully accepted his suffering and focused on his brothers and sisters. All creation was sacred and profoundly holy to him. Francis is said to have composed the "Canticle of the Sun" in late 1224 while recovering from an illness at San Damiano, Italy. A verse from his "Canticle of the Sun" offers joy to all: "We praise You, Lord, for those who pardon, for love of You, bear sickness and trial. Blessed are those who endure in peace, by You Most High, they will be crowned."[22]

We have no control over some losses. The only thing we can do is to be honest with our loss, acknowledge it, and move on, embracing the messiness and uncertainty in our life. We can find powerful comfort in the transforming words of St. Paul to the Romans, 8:38–39, "For I am convinced that neither death, nor life, nor angels, nor rulers, nor things present, nor things to come, nor powers, nor height, nor depth, nor anything else in all creation, will be able to separate us from the love of God in Christ Jesus our Lord."

I hope I can continue to respond to my own physical and professional losses with the grace and generous spirit of Loretta, my mother. She understood that through Christ's birth, power is made manifest through her weakness. We can be transformed by our weakness, our vulnerability during our times of loss.

> Everything can be taken from a man but one thing: the last of the human freedoms— to choose one's attitude in any given set of circumstances, to choose one's own way.[23]
>
> —*Victor Frankl*

To Consider

- Name a loss in your life has profoundly affected you. Did it make you feel powerless? How do you cope with the loss?
- In what ways have you given yourself power over the losses in your life? How have you allowed them to change you for the better?

Prayer

Creator God, maker of earth and my body, help me faithfully embrace the losses in my life and those whom I love. I am vulnerable, and I ask for your loving presence; bless me with the stamina to change these losses into compassion and love. I am before you now standing in all my weakness. Give me the moment of wisdom when I see my trials as a gift of conversion to your love. Change my heart and transform me with your generous love. I ask you to be with me in my time of loss and weakness. Bless me, my God.

1. Available at http://tonysdailyblessings.blogspot.com/2012/04/walk-on-water-wow-quote-for-today-april_7382.html.

2. "Whatsoever You Do," text 1966, 1982, Willard F. Jabusch. Administered by OCP Publications.

3. Dalai Lama, quoted at http://www.goodreads.com/quotes/64768-if-you-have-fear-of-some-pain-or-suffering-you.

4. Robert J. Dufford, S.J. Used by permission of OCP Publications.

5. The Pastoral Care of the Sick, in *The Catholic Handbook for Visiting the Sick and Homebound 2012* (Chicago: Liturgy Training, 2011), pp. 21–22.

6. St. Francis of Assisi, The Rule of the Third Order Regular, 23.

7. Quoted in Kathleen A. Brehony, *After the Darkest Hour: How Suffering Begins the Journey to Wisdom* (New York: Holt, 2001).

8. Text from "You Are Mine" by David Haas. Text Copyright © 1991 by GIA Publications, Inc. All rights reserved. Used by permission.

9. Quoted in Charles W. Gusme, *And You Visited Me: Sacramental Ministry to the Sick and the Dying* (Collegeville, Minn.: Liturgical, 1986).

10. From a talk entitled "Mentally Ill are also made in God's Image," available at www.EWTN.com/library/PAPALDOC/JP96N30.HTM.

11. *The National Directory for Catechesis* (Washington, D.C.: USCCB, 2005), pp. 207–208.

12. Quoted in Gary McGuire, *Realizing Your Potential* (New Delhi, India: Epitome, 2009), p. 108.

13. From www.drvost.com/books.htm.

14. From Prayers for Exercise: Thanksgiving for a Good Workout and Healthy Lifestyle at http://suite101.com/article/prayers-to-exercise-a155575.

15. From www.brainyquote.com/quotes/j/johnfkenn131489.html.

16. From www.bookreviewsandmore.ca/2007_12_01_archive.html.

17. From www.thesunmagazine.org/issues/301/sunbeams.

18. Pope John Paul II, "During the Time of the Jubilee: The Face and Soul of Sports," October 28, 2000.

19. "Walk a Mile in My Shoes," ©1970 Joe South; Sony/ATV Music Publishing LLC.

20. Quoted in Tracy Lewis Tana, *Living Life Consciously* (np: AuthorHouse, 2009), p. 126.

21. Richard Rohr, O.F.M., The Authority of Those Who Have Suffered, available at http://james-sledge.blogspot.com/2010/07/wisdom-from-richard-rohr.html.

22. Francis of Assisi, "Canticle of the Sun," presented by the Kateri Tekakwitha Conservation Center, http://conservation.catholic.org/prayers.htm.

23. Victor Frankl, *Man's Search for Meaning* (New York: Beacon, 2000), p. 75.